Insider Threat

A Guide to Understanding, Detecting, and Defending Against the Enemy from Within

DR. JULIE E. MEHAN, PHD, CISSP, ISSPCS

IT Governance Publishing

Every possible effort has been made to ensure that the information contained in this book is accurate at the time of going to press, and the publisher and the author cannot accept responsibility for any errors or omissions, however caused. Any opinions expressed in this book are those of the author, not the publisher. Websites identified are for reference only, not endorsement, and any website visits are at the reader's own risk. No responsibility for loss or damage occasioned to any person acting, or refraining from action, as a result of the material in this publication can be accepted by the publisher or the author.

Apart from any fair dealing for the purposes of research or private study, or criticism or review, as permitted under the Copyright, Designs and Patents Act 1988, this publication may only be reproduced, stored or transmitted, in any form, or by any means, with the prior permission in writing of the publisher or, in the case of reprographic reproduction, in accordance with the terms of licences issued by the Copyright Licensing Agency. Enquiries concerning reproduction outside those terms should be sent to the publisher at the following address:

IT Governance Publishing
IT Governance Limited
Unit 3, Clive Court
Bartholomew's Walk
Cambridgeshire Business Park
Ely
Cambridgeshire
CB7 4EA
United Kingdom

www.itgovernance.co.uk

© Julie E. Mehan 2016

The author has asserted the rights of the author under the Copyright, Designs and Patents Act, 1988, to be identified as the author of this work.

First published in the United Kingdom in 2016
by IT Governance Publishing.

ISBN: 978-1-84928-839-2

Insider Threat

A Guide to Understanding, Detecting, and Defending Against the Enemy from Within

DEDICATION

This book is dedicated to Jack – ever and always my
anchor, my partner, and my best friend!

PREFACE

After many years in the intelligence community, one of the primary points I learned is that every report should start with the BLUF – Bottom Line Up Front. So here it is: insider threat is real; it is with us daily; it cannot be prevented without a valid insider threat detection, protection, and remediation program.

This book is written as an attempt to understand the environment and psychology that leads an individual from being an insider to becoming an insider threat. The news has recently been full of reporting on the insider threat, and has cast a spotlight on the potential dangers from those in our midst. Many credible security experts warn that any organization can become the target of an insider with an agenda. Understanding the real nature of the insider threat becomes particularly important if we want to look for realistic and enforceable mechanisms for detecting and deterring those that change from insiders to Insider Threats.

In this book, I attempt to address the information environment that enhances the ability of the insider to cause damage, and to provide a body of knowledge useful in acquiring, developing, and sustaining an information environment that may be more resistant to the insider threat. We could not address this issue without including insider threat-based terrorism in the discussion. Nor could this book be of value without addressing the challenges of protecting personal privacy and corporate intellectual property, or the issues associated with an ever-expanding information technology supply chain.

Each chapter concludes with a list of recommendations for additional reading. This book is intended to provide a foundation for developing further education and training curricula and products, as well as being useful to information security practitioners, system administrators, managers, standards developers, evaluators, testers, and those just wishing to be knowledgeable about the establishment and maintenance of an information environment that is more resistant to the insider threat.

The wild growth of the information networks continues to be one of the most remarkable phenomena in human history. They are much more than just a medium for communication – they are at the core of a global information infrastructure that is influencing our culture at the same time as it insinuates itself into our daily lives. There are predictions that this phenomenon is changing everything from standards of literacy and monetary transactions to the practice of medicine. Today, we add the unprecedented growth of social media and information exfiltration to the challenges associated with the expansion of our information environment.

Almost every new development has features that force a balance between positive and negative. For example, the automobile has provided us with new means of effectively and quickly covering distance and moving goods. It has also created pollution and caused innumerable deaths through accident and misuse.

The rapid acceleration of technological change, particularly in the areas of information and information technology, is also not without its benefits and costs. The Internet has become a universal trade space for economic transactions, government decisions, and social interaction. At the same time, the Internet comprises a largely unstructured terrain with challenges as a result of international legal limitations and rules. The result has been a digital wild west, with information networks providing a fertile feeding ground for those who would 'steal' information for reasons ranging from social activism and espionage to profit.

Ray Kurzweil, a noted futurist, wrote several essays about 'The Law of Accelerating Returns', according to which the rate of change in systems, including the growth of information and information technologies, tends to increase exponentially. Kurzweil's analysis of the history of technology appears to indicate that technological change is exponential. In other words, there will not be 100 years of progress in the 21st century – at today's rate of growth, it will actually be more like 20,000 years of progress. There's even exponential growth in the rate of exponential growth.

If we agree on the need to create some form of order in this information growth environment, the application of internationally-accepted laws and regulations is one solution. The other is the proactive implementation of cybersecurity standards and best practices that allow for regularity and fairness in managing the broad issue of insider threat without adversely affecting the cyber environment's open architecture. The idea is to embrace the new information technology as a powerful positive agent for change, without ignoring the dangers created by the deterministic nature of change.

I undertook the task of authoring this book to provide cybersecurity practitioners, managers, and engineers, as well as educators, trainers, and others, with a companion to guide them through the challenge of using national and international standards to address security issues in an environment that is at risk from insider threat. Most recently, I have been a representative on DoD working groups about insider threat and assisted in developing avenues of approach to detect, deter, and defend against insider threat. In the course of this activity, I came to realize how little we really know about the insider, their motivations, and what we can do to facilitate early detection and protection.

The guiding principle behind this book was to have a straightforward discussion about the truth of insiders and insider threat. It is not only about implementing technical cybersecurity solutions – although these are not ignored in the discussion, there are already sufficient works that provide this information. Nor does it focus on insider Threats from specific countries, such as Russia or China. Rather, it is intended to encourage cybersecurity professionals to look at the environment in which our information exists and to view the world of international standards and best practices as a resource for creating a culture of security within their organizations. Our best defense against the insider threat must be found in the establishment of cybersecurity education and awareness, best-of-breed tools and robust policy developed in collaboration between industry, academia and government.

Determining what level of knowledge to assume the readers of this book might possess took several twists and turns. Initially, I took the existence of several significant configuration and technical security guides as a starting point for establishing presumption of knowledge. My goal was – and still is – to provide additional perspective focused on the detection and deterrence of potential insider threats.

Fortunately, efforts to answer the question: 'What are the standards and best practices most relevant to the detection and deterrence of insider threats?' benefited from a number of prior efforts and products. These will be found in the reference lists and further reading sections included at the end of chapters.

The guiding principle is that the book should provide a new perspective on the use of standards and best practices to persons already possessing good security engineering knowledge based on experience and education. Thus I attempted to ensure adequate coverage of requisite knowledge areas in contributing disciplines to enable instructors and professionals from several disciplines, such as software engineering, systems engineering, project management, etc., to identify and acquire competencies associated with the identification and implementation of appropriate standards and best practices.

Finally, I would like to say that I have enjoyed authoring this book, and thank all of the many individuals who provided their knowledge and support in its creation.

Dr. Julie E. Mehan, PhD, CISSP, ISSPCS

ABOUT THE AUTHOR

Dr. Julie Mehan is the Founder and President of JEMStone Strategies and a Principal in a strategic consulting firm in the State of Virginia. She has been a career Government Service employee, a strategic consultant, and an entrepreneur – which either demonstrates her flexibility or inability to hold on to a steady job! She has led business operations, as well as information technology governance and cyber security-related services, including certification and accreditation, systems security engineering process improvement, and cybersecurity strategic planning and program management. During her professional years, she delivered cybersecurity and related privacy services to senior Department of Defense, Federal Government, and commercial clients working in Italy, Australia, Canada, Belgium, Germany, and the United States.

She has served on the President's Partnership for Critical Infrastructure Security, Task Force on Interdependency and Vulnerability Assessments. Dr. Mehan has served as chair for the development of criteria for the International System Security Engineering Professional (ISSEP) certification, as a voting board member for development of the International Systems Security Professional Certification Scheme (ISSPCS), and as Chair of the Systems Certification Working Group of the International Systems Security Engineers Association. Dr. Mehan is also an Associate Professor at the University of Maryland University College, specializing in courses in Cybersecurity, Cyber Terrorism, IT in Organizations and Ethics in an Internet Society.

Dr. Mehan graduated *summa cum laude* with a PhD from Capella University, with dual majors in Organizational

Psychology and Information Technology Management. Her research was focused on success and failure criteria for Chief Information Security Officers (CISOs) in large government and commercial organizations and development of a dynamic model of Chief Security Officer (CSO) leadership. She holds an MA with honors in International Relations Strategy and Law from Boston University, and a BS in History and Languages from the University of New York. Dr. Mehan was elected 2003 Woman of Distinction by the Women of Greater Washington and has published numerous articles including Framework for Reasoning About Security – A Comparison of the Concepts of Immunology and Security; System Dynamics, Criminal Behavior Theory and Computer-Enabled Crime; The Value of Information-Based Warfare To Affect Adversary Decision Cycles; and Information Operations in Kosovo: Mistakes, Missteps, and Missed Opportunities, released in Cyberwar 4.0.

Dr. Mehan is the author of two books published by ITGP: *Cyberwar, CyberTerror, CyberCrime and CyberActivism*, 2nd Edition published in 2014, and *The Definitive Guide to the Certification & Accreditation Transformation*, published in 2009.

Dr. Mehan is particularly proud of her past engagement as pro-bono President of Warrior to Cyber Warrior (W2CW) (*http://warrior2cyberwarrior.org/index.html*), a non-profit organization dedicated to providing cost-free career transition training to veterans and Wounded Warriors returning from the various military campaigns of recent years.

Dr. Mehan is fluent in German and has conversational skills in French and Italian.

The author can be contacted at *je.mehan@outlook.com*.

ACKNOWLEDGEMENTS

An outstanding team of dedicated professionals contributed to the creation and publication of this book. My primary contacts at ITGP, Ms. Vicki Utting and Ms. Alexandra Thurman, have enthusiastically supported this book – as well as the others published by ITGP – and played a large role in shaping the final products. Editor Rob Coston polished the prose and provided many excellent suggestions that made the book easier to read.

I would like to thank Antonio Velasco, Maarten Souw and Giuseppe G. Zorzino for their helpful comments during the review process.

I am also thankful to all of those who provided valuable, usable insight into the Insider Threat problem. I cannot call them out by name. But you know who you are!

CONTENTS

Contents

LIST OF FIGURES

List of Figures

LIST OF TABLES

INTRODUCTION

We have met the enemy and he is us. – Walt Kelly in *Pogo**

It's an unfortunate fact, but nations, companies, and individuals have frequently been betrayed by individuals in positions of trust – also known as insiders – and for a long time, the insider threat has largely been ignored in favor of the external hacker. Why? The external hacker is easier to detect, easier to control, and it is much more visible than the enemy from within. The reality is that insider threat activities have been occurring for a very long time and are still taking place but, since these attacks occur *within* the organization, they take place in private. High-profile public attacks are difficult to deny; the private attacks by insiders are much easier to hide.

In recent years, however, thanks to individuals such as Edward Snowden and Private Chelsea (Bradley) Manning, discussions at all levels about insider threat have become increasingly prevalent. insider threat is not fiction; it is real, it is happening more than we know and – if not taken seriously – it can cause serious damage.

The key concept to remember about insider threat is that, generally speaking, insiders will take advantage of chinks in the armor of the organization – the ones that give them

---

* *Pogo* refers to the title and main character of a cartoon strip created by Walt Kelly. The quote, which appeared in 1953, paraphrases a message from US Navy Commodore Perry in 1813 which stated: "We have met the enemy and they are ours."

the greatest opportunity for success and the least likelihood that they will be detected.

The broad view is that individuals in positions of trust within an organization – and more importantly, with access to its facilities, its information and its information infrastructure – have the ability to inflict significant harm should they decide to 'go rogue' for whatever reasons. Insiders can take advantage of the fact that they are already within the security perimeter and already have knowledge of how the organization does business.

In response, the US Government has issued a number of mandates designed to increase awareness and to establish standards for insider threat programs across all federal agencies. These include executive order 13587, Structural Reforms to Improve the Security of Classified Networks and the Responsible Sharing and Safeguarding of Classified Information, signed in October 2011, and the National Insider Threat Policy and Minimum Standards for Executive Branch Insider Threat Programs, signed in November 2012. Since the issuance of these documents, US federal agencies have paid significant attention to the creation of insider threat mitigation programs.

Despite this laser-like attention of federal agencies on the insider threat problem, less has been done in the private sector. Much of the critical infrastructure in the US and other nations is in the hands of private companies, including the communications and technology infrastructure over which most of the important and sensitive – or even classified – work is done. Insider Threats in the private sector can be very damaging, with results ranging from a loss of confidence in the products or reputation of the organization to loss of market share, loss of future earnings resulting from the theft of intellectual property, damage to economic viability, or even the compromising of the infrastructure – all of which can have a negative impact on national, as well as corporate, security.

Before we really enter into the discussion about insider threat, it's important to start with a definition of the insider and insider threat. The definition of an insider generally refers to current, former, or contract employees or affiliates of an organization. The National Counterintelligence and Security Center (NCSC) defines insider threat as arising " when a person with authorized access to... resources, to include personnel, facilities, information, equipment, networks, and systems, uses that access to harm the security of the... organization. Malicious insiders can inflict incalculable damage."[1]

> "The whole Insider Threat phenomenon, they act like it's a new thing." Tess Schrodinger, Cybersecurity Expert, at the 2014 DefCon.

Insiders are not just employees; today they can include contractors, business partners, auditors or even an alumnus with a valid email address. And not all insider attacks are malicious; the perpetrators may be unknowing pawns of a malevolent colleague or a poorly-tested system, or simply the careless initiator of unintended consequences – thus creating an unintentional insider threat. But one thing is clear – Insider threats are a costly problem, bedeviling organizations that lack the resources to monitor actions, prevent bad outcomes, or avoid harm when data leakages occur.

Let's start with one fact: even though it seems that everyone is talking about insider threat now, *it is not a new threat!* Although most of the conversations about insider threat today focus on access to digital information, the insider problem predates information systems by hundreds of years. In fact, the insider problem predates computers by thousands of years.

There has been a string of insider threats long before Edward Snowden's and Bradley Manning's famous leaks, ranging from Guy Fawkes – who tried to blow up Britain's House of Lords – to Brian Patrick Regan, an American Air Force sergeant convicted of trying to sell secrets to Saddam Hussein. And if we want to take it all the way back to Biblical times, we can even cite Judas as an insider threat. In each case, the individual exhibited what we now know to be identifiable signs of a threat – but the signs went unreported because of the unwillingness or inability of colleagues to accept the possibility that this trusted individual might really be a danger to themselves or the organization.

But today, with the vast amount of information stored on information systems, the impact of a data compromise by an insider can approach an unparalleled level. This is never more evident than when one considers the international impact of the massive exfiltration and release of data perpetrated by Edward Snowden, perhaps the most notorious of recent insiders. As damaging as some of Snowden's disclosures were, the US and other nations were already dealing with the fact that they had been victimized by another insider just a couple of years earlier by Chelsea (formerly Private Bradley) Manning and the release of data through WikiLeaks.

Arguably, a trusted insider can cause more damage than the trained, foreign intelligence officer working on behalf of a government or organization. In the corporate world, most employers think of the negative consequences of making a wrong hire in terms of "is this person a fit for the team, do they appear to be productive, and will they be good with customers?" But what type of background checks do they actually do? Most are limited to credit checks, drug history, past employers, criminal background, driving records and now social media sites. Once a prospective employee passes these checks, they are often completely trusted. But does this mean that the employee is loyal to the company?

US federal agencies and the Department of Defense (DoD) may conduct more extensive background investigations, but once these are complete, the employee is trusted. Snowden, Manning and other recent insiders all exhibited traits that should have aroused some level of concern with their employers, but what really happens? It's called the ostrich approach – if I'm not sure, or don't like what I see, I'll bury my head in the sand and pretend the problem isn't there. According to Mac Thornberry*: "To stick our head in the sand and pretend we are somehow safer if we do not know, or to pretend we are somehow safer… seems to me not only foolish, but actually dangerous."[2]

Or, even more to the point, this quote from Herbie Mann*, noted musician: "I always say, if you keep your head in the sand, you don't know where the kick's coming from."[3]

Even if the organization has taken its head out of the sand and acknowledges that insiders present an increasing security risk, the problem is still being disregarded by some organizations. Dr. Eric Cole attributes this to three key reasons:

1. They don't know it's happening.
2. They fear bad publicity.
3. They find it easier to be in denial.[4]

Is it possible to detect or defend against the enemy from within? While there are efforts underway to improve the means of detecting and defeating the insider threat, research also indicates that there are deep organizational and cognitive biases that cause both co-workers and managers to downplay the threats insiders pose to their facilities and operations.

Difficult to detect and prevent, attacks by people with legitimate access to an organization's computers and networks represent a growing problem in our digital world. These insider threats frustrate employers who lack the resources to identify potential perpetrators and monitor their behavior. Dr. David Charney, who has conducted extensive research into the psychology of the insider, noted: "Over the years, government intelligence agencies have made significant efforts to pre-emptively screen away prospective traitors. Nevertheless, all the world's intelligence

---

* Herbie Mann, born Herbert Solomon, was a well-known jazz musician who played both the flute and the tenor saxophone.

services have suffered penetrations, including our own. Increasingly stringent security practices, such as more frequent follow-up background investigations, have been used to lessen the threat of insider spies. Americans have particularly favored advanced technology solutions. Nevertheless, these heroic measures seem to fail time and again... Strongly motivated spies have demonstrated the capacity to successfully discern the seams between the most well thought out protective measures – and have insidiously slipped right through."[5]

So, how can we detect, deter, or maybe even prevent the insider threat? While technical solutions may be useful on the edges, at its core insider threat is a human problem that requires human solutions.

CHAPTER 1: THE HIDDEN THREAT

Someone once told me that none of us are actually afraid of the dark; we're scared of what it conceals from us. We're afraid of having something with the potential to hurt us standing right before our eyes and not registering it as a threat. – Unknown[6]

In the past few years, we have witnessed an almost continuous flow of loss and data theft, as governments and businesses have had to admit their security and data protection weaknesses. The impact of these events on reputation and brand, as well as the legal ramifications for high profile organizations, has been broad and damaging. There is now a greater understanding that the hidden rogue insider can cause extreme harm.

The narcissistic co-worker who requires constant attention and validation could well be a high-performing, trustworthy, valuable member of an organization. The non-social co-worker who avoids contact could be just a highly skilled, but introverted employee. Or they could each represent a hidden threat – the insider who may deliberately or inadvertently cause damage to the entire organization.

> "The damages caused by malicious insiders each year are not only substantial, but also on the rise." INSA Cyber Insider Threat Subcouncil

Why The Insider Threat is Called 'The Hidden Threat'

Insiders have a unique ability to cause harm because an organization's internal security measures – if they exist at all – are generally easier to circumvent than their hardened perimeter defenses. From their positions within an organization's offices and networks, insiders not only have enhanced access to their targets, they also have the ability to identify any lapses in technological protections and policy enforcement, and thus increased opportunity to discover where the critical information assets are located and how to get to them without risking detection. Insider Threats may also include well-intentioned employees who unwittingly cause or contribute to a security incident.

Regardless of whether the employee is an unintentional or intentional threat, the Software Engineering Institute at Carnegie Mellon* discovered that approximately 85% of insider compromises were performed by employees of the victim organization after reviewing more than 800 insider threat cases. Contractors, subcontractors and trusted business partners made up the other 15%. In fact, the author Brian Contos emphasized the fact that most threats are conducted by those we trust the most by calling the insider threat "The Enemy at the Water Cooler."[7]

Looking for threats from the inside may be one of the hardest things for an organization to do, since most do not want to admit that a trusted employee could or would

---

* The Computer Emergency Response Team (CERT) group at the Carnegie Mellon University Software Engineering Institute (CMU SEI) have been researching insider threat since 2002. The CERT Insider Threat Center has built an extensive library and comprehensive database containing more than 600 cases of crimes committed against organizations by insiders, and is a treasure-trove of resources for understanding and combating insider threat.

intentionally or unintentionally cause harm. Most organizations focus too much attention towards attacks originating from the outside and less towards those that may come from the inside. Therefore, the insider threat quickly becomes a hidden threat.

Defining the Insider

Research into the insider threat problem has been complicated by the lack of a precise definition of an insider, which leaves researchers subject to their own definition of situation, biases, and assumptions. The challenge is made more complex by the assumption that the boundary or perimeter can be clearly defined, so that anyone inside the security boundary is consequently an insider. The idea of a distinct perimeter has been blurred even more today through the increase in mobile computing, teleworking, outsourcing, and contracting. Moreover, today's discussions about insider threat tend to focus on the network perimeter and fail to fully consider physical boundaries. Despite the difficulty of defining a boundary, definitions of insider threat are still largely focused on a perimeter-based definition of who should be considered an insider. For example, take a look at this definition of an insider: an "individual who has, or previously had been, authorized to use the information systems they employed to perpetrate harm."[8]

One of the research bodies examining insider threat, CMU SEI, has evolved perhaps the most comprehensive yet simple definition – one that isn't bound by the definition of a perimeter: *The person who has the potential to harm an organization for which they have inside knowledge or access.*[9]

One common thread runs through all of the definitions – access. So, let's look at another definition from the National Infrastructure Advisory Council (NIAC) that broadens the digital lens: *An insider threat is one or more individuals with the access and/or insider knowledge of a company, an organization or an enterprise, that would allow them the opportunity to exploit weaknesses in that organization's facilities, security, systems, products, or services, with the intent to cause harm or to obtain an unauthorized advantage.*[10]

Insiders are not just employees: by focusing on the concept of access, the group can be expanded to include contractors, business partners, auditors – even an alumnus with a valid email address. Insider knowledge allows the potential insider threat group to be expanded to include former members who may lack access in the present, but who have historical knowledge of organizational security practices and weaknesses.

And not all insider attacks are malicious; the perpetrators may be unknowing pawns of a malevolent colleague, users of a poorly-tested system, or simply the careless initiator of unintended consequences. But one thing is clear: Insider threats are a costly problem, bedeviling organizations that lack the resources to monitor actions, prevent bad outcomes, or avoid harm when data leakages occur. In a 2001 paper, Maglaras and Furnell[11] provided a visual categorization of intentional versus unintentional threat (*Figure 1*).

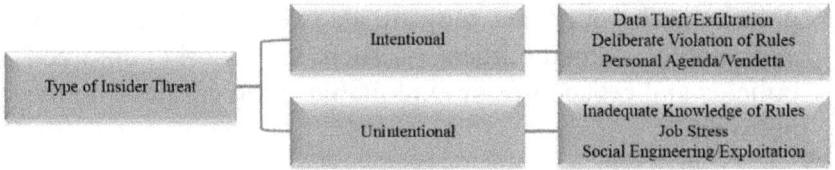

Figure 1: Intentional vs. unintentional threat

The lack of a comprehensive definition of the insider threat leads organizations to think that insider threat can be prevented through the use of a policy, or by creating a defensible network perimeter, but both have inherent limitations: some policies cannot be fully or even partially implemented, leaving an organization vulnerable to security lapses. Additionally, most users of information systems tend to have move privileges than are essential to completing their assigned tasks. Finally, the creation of a hardened network perimeter does nothing to prevent an insider from doing damage.

One thing is beyond doubt: an insider can cause significant damage to the organization, regardless of whether the attack is a low level theft of proprietary information or a technically sophisticated act of sabotage. Insiders are a hidden threat because they may be able to elude detection as they bypass the physical and technical security measures intended to prevent unauthorized access. Any insider attack has the potential to weaken or destroy public trust, share value, or financial solvency – they can slowly erode or quickly destroy the foundations of an organization. The standard perimeter defenses, such as electronic physical access systems, firewalls, and intrusion detection systems exist primarily to defend against the external threat. The insider is not only aware of the organization's security policies and procedures, they are also very cognizant of any exploitable vulnerabilities – such as poorly enforced policies and procedures or exploitable technical flaws in the network.

Although some of the most publicized insider threat events have taken place in the US, the problem of insider threat is also global in scale. In 2013, a German telecommunications provider announced that the data of two million of its customers was compromised by an insider. A UK-based supermarket chain was attacked by another insider in 2013, who posted personal details of the employees' bank accounts. These are just two of numerous examples of insider threat worldwide.

Insider Threat Has Many Forms

Recent news events lead us to think that the insider threat has only one form – the theft of data – but in reality, the insider has many ways of striking at an organization: sabotage, fraud, intellectual property (IP) theft, and government and industrial data leaks or breaches. Some cases of malicious activity fall into multiple categories. For example, the Insider Threat Study conducted jointly by the US Secret Service and the Computer Emergency Response Team (CERT) saw several cases where an employee committed an act of sabotage against their employer's systems, and then offered to assist them in the recovery efforts for a sum of money – extortion. One case involved three categories of insider activity: the insider quit his job after an argument, but was offered no severance package. He made an unauthorized copy of an application he was developing, deleted the application code from the library, and stole all of the backup tapes. He then offered to restore the content to the application library for $50,000. He was charged and convicted of the crime, but the company never recovered all of the application code – a major setback for the organization.[12]

When discussing insider threat, most of us immediately look at banking, financial services, government, healthcare, or manufacturing as the activities with the most probability of an insider attack, but other organizations and businesses may also be affected. According to a 2014 survey by SpectorSoft, 37% of data attacks in real estate were from insiders, in the public sector 24%, in administrative organizations 27%, and in mining 25%. The inescapable conclusion is that every type of organization can be vulnerable to some type of insider abuse, error, or malicious attack that can impact reputation, operations and profitability, expose data, harm the organization, or deliver valuable intellectual property into the hands of competitors.[13]

As this book was being written, there were a number of terrorist attacks. On 13 November 2015, a series of coordinated terrorist attacks were conducted in Paris. More than 100 individuals were killed and more than 300 were injured. It was the deadliest attack on French soil since World War II and the news staggered the world. The attackers came from inside France. Not three weeks later, 14 people were killed and 21 wounded when a husband and wife couple engaged in a gun massacre during an office Christmas party in San Bernardino, California. As in the previous instance, the attackers were insiders – many of those killed were colleagues of one of the attackers. As a result of these events, and others, the insider threat category of terrorist acts was added to the list.

Sabotage

Sabotage* is defined by Oxford Dictionaries as the "deliberate destruction, damage, or obstruction, especially for political or military advantage."[14] The saboteur is the insider who intends to harm their organization, rather than simply steal company resources or information. Insider sabotage can take several forms – physical harm to the organization, economic damage, and IT sabotage.

Sabotage by insiders is not new. In fact, it may be one of the earliest forms of insider threat. Physical and economic forms of sabotage have long been with us. One of the first formal uses of the term sabotage appeared in the 1830s, when a French book entitled *Sabotage* promulgated various means of sabotage used by European radicals since that time. In wartime, sabotage is one of the most effective weapons in any nation's arsenal. During World War I, insiders planted by the German Government blew up the munitions supply terminal at the Black Tom pier in New York Harbor. The organization known as Industrial Workers of the World (IWW) justified sabotage as a by-product of class struggle, a means to gain better conditions for workers.

Sabotage in the workplace is one of the more common forms of sabotage, and it is not limited to destruction of the physical facility or damage to the IT infrastructure. The damage can take many forms, such as:

- deliberate non-performance;
- falsification of company records;

---

* The term "sabotage" is often said to derive from actions taken by French factory workers to jam loom machinery with wooden shoes called "sabots."

- spread of untrue rumors with the intent to cause damage to the company, other employees, or property;
- damaging key parts of machinery or other equipment;
- using materials or weapons to destroy or damage organizational property;
- using arson, vandalism, or destructive pranks.

In the 49 cases studied by the CMU SEI, losses were as high as tens of millions; 75% experienced an impact to their business operations. (Source: *Management and Education of the Risk of Insider Threat (MERIT): Mitigating the Risk of Sabotage to Employers' Information, Systems or Networks)*

IT Sabotage

IT sabotage, on the other hand, is a relatively new form and is focused on negatively affecting or damaging an organization's information systems. Recent events have raised the public's awareness of IT-related forms of sabotage. Although there are many reasons for an insider to execute an act of IT sabotage, most acts are committed by a technical employee who uses their knowledge of the organization's IT infrastructure to sabotage systems or networks in retaliation for a perceived work-related slight.

Here is just one of many examples of IT sabotage committed by an insider: In December of 2006, a former employee of the Fortune 100 financial company UBS PaineWebber, Roger Duronio, was sentenced to 97 months in prison and more than $3 million in restitution for committing an act of IT sabotage. Why? He didn't receive the large annual bonus he expected. Duronio, a system administrator with privileged access to the network, planted a logic bomb that took down about 2,000 servers in the central data center when the script activated. The timing was intentional – the script activated just at the opening of the stock market for the day. Over 17,000 brokers were unable to make any trades.[15] His goal was to cause the company's stock to fall.

Duronio is representative of the typical insider threat who perpetrates an act of IT sabotage. He was disgruntled and wanted revenge for a perceived work-related slight; he demonstrated troubling behavior prior to the attack; he held a technical position; and he left just before the attack launched.

According to research by the CMU SEI CERT, the most common types of IT sabotage include:

- developing a script or program, such as a logic bomb*, then creating a backdoor account for later use to initiate the script or including a time for activation in the script;
- planting a virus on organization or customer information systems;
- installation of remote system administration tools that would allow the insider to enter the system and either steal information or damage the systems.

Whether it is physical, reputational or IT sabotage, the primary reasons for insider sabotage are generally the same. Sabotage is usually rationalized as a course of action when

---

* A logic bomb, also called slag code because all that's left after it detonates is computer slag, is not the same thing as a virus, although it often behaves in a similar manner. It is a piece of computer code that executes a malicious task, such as clearing a hard drive or deleting specific files, when it is triggered by a specific event. It's secretly inserted into the code of a computer's existing software, where it lies dormant until that event occurs. Retrieved from How Stuff Works: *http://computer.howstuffworks.com/logic-bomb.htm*.

an individual believes that the organization or someone within the organization has done them wrong in some way.

Fraud

Research by The Security Company* has indicated that the lure of committing fraud is likely to increase in times of economic recession, which are frequently accompanied by unemployment, job worries, higher personal debt, and a rising cost of living. In 2008-2009, the global community experienced a deep recession that wreaked economic havoc in most of the developed nations. Although we are gradually emerging from the worst of this recession, there are still many lasting effects. One of these is a noticeable increase in fraudulent activity. Oxford Dictionaries defines fraud as "wrongful or criminal deception intended to result in financial or personal gain."[16]

> In 2014, approximately 277,000 acts of insider fraudulent activity were reported – a **25%** increase over 2013 – with an estimated loss of $3.7 trillion. (Source: CIFAS)

According to CIFAS*, which focuses on fraud in the UK, fraudulent activity across all sectors has been steadily increasing by a rate of more than 40% in the last few years.[17] The most common cause of insider fraud is pure

---

* The Security Company is a UK firm providing employee security awareness training and education.
* CIFAS is a not-for profit organization working in the UK, whose mission is to deter, detect and prevent fraud and fraud-related crime. The organization focuses on harnessing data and technology and works in partnership with its more than 330 members from insurance, telecommunications and the public sector.

greed, and the most disturbing fact is that the true scale of insider fraud is unknown.

> The FBI estimates that insiders steal eight times more money through fraud than is stolen through bank robberies.

The US Office of Thrift Supervision (OTS)* published an update to its Fraud Examination Handbook in May 2010[18] to include insider fraud. This update occurred in response to a noticeable increase in fraud and insider abuse tied to the downturns in the market starting in 2007. OTS identified several primary forms of insider fraud:

- **Identity theft** – the unauthorized transfer or use or another person's identity with the intent to obtain illegal profit. Identity theft is made much easier by the fact that our personal information is found in so many locations. Most of the identity theft is conducted by individuals in positions of trust that work in the very companies that handle or process our information. Desperate people can do desperate things – and the theft of personal data for profit is an increasingly popular crime of opportunity.

- **Mortgage fraud** – the illegal or unauthorized attempt to obtain financial advantage by misrepresentation, to carry out fraud for profit or fraud for housing. Fraud for profit is usually conducted by financial industry insiders, using their specialized knowledge and access to obtain material profit from a fraudulent mortgage scheme.

---

* The Office of Thrift Supervision (OTS) was established by the US Congress in 1989 to address the protection of US financial institutions.

Fraud for housing typically represents actions by a borrower, who seeks to obtain home ownership under false pretenses. According to the OTS, mortgage fraud has increased 95.62% since 2007.[19]

- **Check fraud** – the illegal or unauthorized use of personal or business checks to obtain financial profit. Types of check fraud range from forged signatures, forged endorsements, counterfeit checks and altered checks to check kiting.* The US Department of the Treasury estimates that 1.2 million fraudulent checks are written annually in the US, resulting in losses of well over $1 billion every year.[20]

- **Credit/Debit card fraud** – theft or fraud committed using a payment card, such as a credit or debit card, as a source of profit. Like many of the other financial fraud types, credit/debit card fraud is primarily conducted by trusted insiders and is often linked with identity theft. Credit/debit card fraud has evolved from theft of the card itself to the use of card skimmers to capture card data. In the US, an estimated $788 million is lost to debit card fraud alone.[21]

Theft of Intellectual Property (IP)

According to a Symantec survey, intellectual property theft is most often conducted by trusted insiders – otherwise known as *frenemy** #*1*.[22] Some insider activities involved the theft of information to sell to a company's competitor, others were conducted by disgruntled staff who wanted to publicly

---

* Check kiting is the process of depositing a check from one bank account into a second bank account without sufficient funds.
* 'Frenemy' is a colloquial term referring to an individual who may be both a friend and an enemy.

embarrass their employer, and some occurred because the insider wanted to help a friend or family member. What is most startling is the sheer number of insiders who do not consider the theft of corporate data to be unethical, much less criminal. "62% of employees think it's acceptable to transfer corporate data to their personal computers, tablets, smart phones and Cloud-sharing apps. 56% don't think it's a crime to use trade secrets taken from a previous employer."[23] And it's not only employees that commit theft of IP – in fact, trusted business partners accounted for more than 17% of insider theft of IP.[24]

Often, insiders felt they were entitled to the information they stole, some because they had been at least partially involved in the development of the IP. Entitlement is a thread that runs through a number of insider threat cases. Dissatisfaction, often resulting from denial of a request for promotion or preference, was another primary justification for insider theft of IP. The dissatisfaction caused by the denial of the request led to an increasing loss of employee loyalty to the organization.

Several hypotheses have emerged as a result of research:

- insiders who stole IP often demonstrated signs of job dissatisfaction;
- the stolen IP was most often within their area of responsibility and, in many cases, the insiders were directly involved in its development;
- the IP was usually stolen within the first month of a resignation;
- explicit deception was most likely if the insider had previously executed a non-disclosure agreement (NDA).

Research by the CMU SEI indicated that the execution of an NDA by employees was no guarantee that they would not engage in insider threat activities. In fact, 41% of the insiders stole information despite having signed IP agreements with the company.[25]

Impacts as a result of the theft of IP include reputational losses or financial damage so extensive that companies were forced to lay off employees or even close down operations. CMU SEI research indicated that the cost of IP theft was over $1 million in 48% of the cases and over $100,000 in 71% of the cases studied.[26]

In addition to IP theft by employees, CMU SEI also studied cases that involved theft of IP inside the U.S. by foreign governments or organizations. These cases differ because the "insiders may have a sense of duty or loyalty to their countries of birth that overrides any loyalty to their employer."[27] Research into the case studies also suggests that some foreign entities may even assist the insiders in stealing IP. One of these case studies involves Wen Chyu Lin, a research scientist, who was convicted in 2011 of stealing IP from his US employer and selling it to companies in his home country of China. He not only stole secrets himself, he also conspired with other Chinese national employees of the company to steal corporate information, paying one partner-in-crime $50,000 for a process manual.[28]

Since many cases of foreign insider theft of IP lie outside the jurisdiction of US law enforcement entities, it is even more difficult for an organization to limit damage as a result of the theft. The insider may leave the US, making it difficult or even impossible to find, detain and arrest him/her.* Most perpetrators stole the IP to gain an advantage for their

---

* CMU SEI studied 29 cases; 27 involved male insiders.

country of origin, a competitor, or to create a new business for themselves. The motivations were generally classed as either internal or external as illustrated in *Figure 2* below.

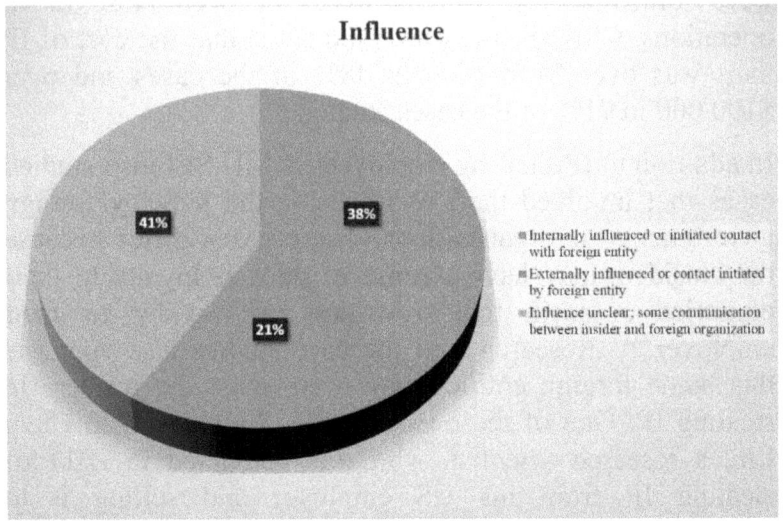

Figure 2: Percentage of external influence in foreign theft of IP

Government and Industry Data Leaks/Breaches

Although the theft of intellectual property could be considered a form of data leak, the massive breaches in recent years require organizations to address this as a unique and serious concern with its own unique characteristics. Insider attacks and external hackers have recently been grabbing headlines; however, these reports barely scratch the surface of the real extent of insider threat activity. In fact, unless you've been on the moon, the names Snowden, WikiLeaks*, Julian Assange and Bradley Manning should certainly be familiar – or, at least, you've heard them at once or twice.

Despite increased awareness of insider threat and associated efforts at establishing defensive measures, "a rise in inside threats has been observed and particularly in incidents of data leakage."[29] According to a survey by SafeNet*, the worldwide "pace of compromised data in Q1 [2014] amounted to *approximately 93,000 records per hour,* a 233% increase over the same quarter in 2013."[30] Research by the Ponemon Institute concluded that each lost record cost approximately $204 to restore. So, considering the number above – the loss of 93,000 records – the global cost equals approximately $18,972,000 per hour![31]

Data leaks and breaches are not exclusively focused on the US. The top spot actually belongs to South Korea with four of the top five breaches worldwide in 2014 and a loss of over 158 million records – 79% of the total number of reported data record losses. During the same period, 13% of the total reported incidents occurred in Europe.[32]

Whether or not they are malicious, data leaks and breaches hurt organizations. They can damage reputation, impact market position, and cost millions of dollars in actual losses and the costs of reparation. So, why is this occurring? "Companies [and governments] are producing an ever-

---

* WikiLeaks was founded by Australian national Julian Assange, in 2006. Assange himself was known as a journalist, publisher, computer programmer and hacker. He allegedly established WikiLeaks to expose the activities of governments and corporations and inform the public.
* SafeNet is an international company specializing in cryptographic encryption and data protection.

growing pile of digital information… Keeping tabs on it all is increasingly hard, not only because there is so much of it, but also because of the ease of storing and sending it."[33]

Years ago, when information was kept only in paper form, it was much easier to control and protect than in today's digital, interconnected environment. Add to this the advent of mobile devices and social media, and we have instant communication and instant sharing of information. This migration is not just affecting the corporate sector; it has had a similar effect on facilitating government data leaks. In 2013, US Army Private Bradley (Chelsea) Manning was sentenced to 35 years in prison for stealing more than 700,000 government and military data files and providing them to WikiLeaks. This gigantic data leak exposed US and other nations' military and diplomatic activities around the world.

Figure 3 below shows the approximate percentage of each of the above discussed forms of insider threat activity.

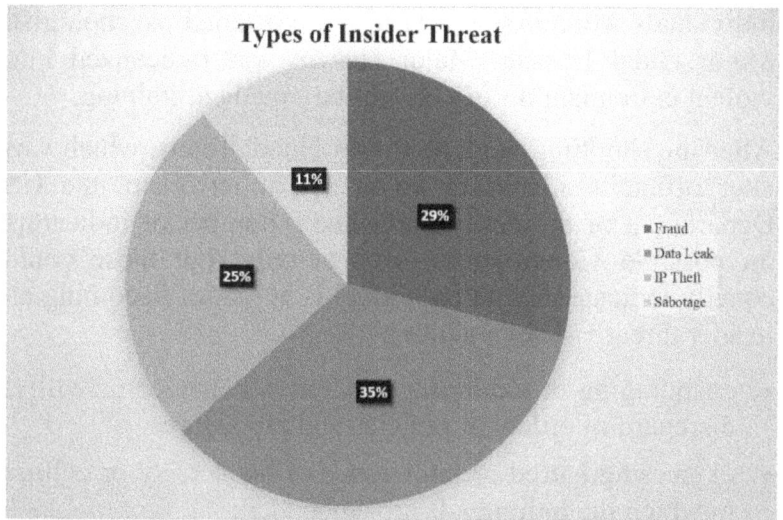

Figure 3: Percentage of insider threat by type

Terrorist Attack – Another Form of Insider Threat

In 2015, the threat of insider terrorism, also known as homegrown terrorism, became a stark reality for several nations. The terrorist attacks in Paris in August 2015, and those in San Bernardino, California, in November 2015, have served to magnify our international sense of vulnerability. According to Gordon Lederman, "an individual within [any nation] segregated within his or her own community of sympathizers, can potentially radicalize to violent extremism and then utilize modern technology to kill people or hobble critical infrastructure."[34] Since 2009, there have been more than 30 cases of homegrown terrorism in the US alone. While some were stopped before any damage could be done, others went undetected until it was too late. On 5 November 2009, 12 members of the US military and one government civilian were killed and 32 individuals wounded by a U.S. Army-trained psychologist, Major Nidal Hassan. Major Hassan was radicalized into violent extremism during his military medical training.

After the shooting incident at Fort Hood, Texas, which was later officially identified as an act of terrorism, the US Department of the Army published a number of indicators on possible violent or terrorist activity, but these could equally indicate that an individual is at risk of becoming an insider threat.[35] They include:

- encouraging or exhibiting disruptive behavior or willful disregard of orders or policies and procedures;
- expressing hatred or intolerance of the society or culture in which the individuals are embedded;
- expressing sympathy for organizations or individuals that encourage violence;
- exhibiting extreme anxiety;
- associating with or expressing support for known terrorists or terrorist organizations;
- browsing or participating in online sites that advocate violence and contain terrorist propaganda or literature;
- vocalizing support for the use of violence to achieve political/religious/ideological goals;
- obtaining financial or other material support from a terrorist organization, or providing such support to a terrorist organization;
- membership in violent, extremist or terrorist groups;
- purchasing a large number of weapons, ammunition and bomb-making materials;
- participating in training with radical or extremist organizations, either within or outside their native country;

- having ties to known extremists, radicals, terrorist groups and/or their supporters;
- termination of employment or non-selection for promotion, bonus, or other expected recognition.

One of the most significant fears is that of an insider threat to nuclear facilities. "All of the cases of theft of nuclear materials where the circumstances of the theft are known were perpetrated either by insiders or with the help of insiders."[36] The thought of a terrorist-associated attack on a nuclear facility or using nuclear materials is the stuff that keeps one awake at night.

Otto von Bismarck* remarked: "It is said that only a fool learns from his own mistakes; a wise man from the mistakes of others." Nuclear facilities and operations should learn from the insider threats described above that affect other sectors, such as finance and government, and address the deep organizational and cognitive biases that lead them to downplay or even hide the insider threat to nuclear facilities and activities.

Recommendations for additional reading
Gordon Lederman and Kate Martin. *Patriots Debate: Contemporary Issues in National Security Law, Second Edition.* Published by the American Bar Association, Standing Committee on Law and National Security, 2012.
Blackwell, Clive. *The Insider Threat: Combatting the Enemy Within.* 7 April 2009. IT Governance Publishing.

---

* Otto von Bismarck was the Prime Minister of Prussia and later the founder and first chancellor from 1871–1890 of the German Empire.

Brian T. Contos. *Enemy at the Water Cooler: Real Life Stories of Inside Threats and Enterprise Security Management Countermeasures*. Syngress Publishing, Inc. 2006.

CHAPTER 2: INSIDER THREAT MODELS AND INDICATORS

I believe in rules. Sure I do. If there weren't any rules, how could I break them? – Leo Durocher*[37]

Recent research into insider threat modelling by such organizations as the Carnegie Mellon University Software Engineering Institute (CMU SEI) and the UK's Centre for the Protection of National Infrastructure (CPNI) has resulted in a more comprehensive picture of possible indications and warnings, observables, and actions to mitigate the threat. This section includes case studies of insider threat drawn from history and recent events.

There is no single profile of an individual who is likely to develop into an insider threat. insider threats do not carry a sign or have a mark on their forehead. They certainly do not announce their intent to execute damaging actions. However, assessments of individuals who have committed insider threat activities have allowed research organizations to identify a number of behavioral characteristics and personality traits that appear over and over again in individuals who have later been identified as an insider threat.

Before we continue to a discussion of insider threat models and indicators, let's look at the various ways in which insiders can be categorized based on the environment from which an insider threat emerges.

---

* Leo Durocher was an early 19th century American professional baseball player. He was often called 'Leo the Lip'.

As we review these categories of insiders, consider also how the environment has evolved through the ages – from a fairly primitive structure focused on the physical world to the digital world we know today – and how this evolution has influenced the power of the insider. Those operating in the older setting could be called "bricks and mortar"* insiders[38].

The Bricks and Mortar Insider

There are countless historical examples of the impact of the "bricks and mortar" insider. In the past, these individuals were most likely to be called saboteurs or spies, but in reality bricks and mortar insiders provide the first historical examples of an insider threat. These insiders – or these saboteurs – are often employees who intend to harm something or someone in an organization. Like the digital insider, they may feel disgruntled or taken for granted, and believe they are not getting enough of the company 'perks', or they may be following a personal agenda of revenge or punishment for a real or perceived ill.

Critical infrastructure such as bridges, electricity generation facilities, water purification or nuclear power plants presents a prime opportunity for the insider. Insider threats to critical infrastructure are certainly nothing new – just think of saboteurs in the First and Second World Wars – but the environment has changed to meet new economic realities. Not only employees, but also vendors, contractors, and business partners have access to critical infrastructure facilities.

---

* This designation was used in a presentation delivered by Dr. Michael Gelles and Dr. Jesse Goldhammer at the RSA Conference held in April 2015 in San Francisco. Its use here is adapted to cover a longer, but equally relevant, period of history in terms of the insider threat.

In August 2014, an insider attack at the Marshal Fahim National Defense University training center in Kabul resulted in the death of Major General Harold Green, the most senior US military officer killed in action since the Vietnam War. Seven US and five British soldiers were also injured in the attack. The attacker was a soldier attending the training center who opened fire with his US-issued M16 rifle from a guard post within the coalition base.[39] The motive: political retribution.

Hard Copy-Based Insider

The hard copy-based insider is another example of the concept that insider threat has deep historical roots. In early days – and even today – much of the insider threat focused on espionage and the theft of actual documents of an industrial, economic, political or military nature. One of the earliest recorded cases of industrial espionage took place in 1712, when Father Francois Xavier d'Entrecolles, a French Jesuit missionary in China, was given access by Catholic converts to the royal Chinese porcelain manufacturer in the secret city of Jingdezhen. He learned the process and transmitted secret documents back to France revealing the long-secret methods of Chinese porcelain manufacture. The result: Chinese domination of the porcelain industry came to an end.[40] The primary motive was ideology and loyalty to his nation of origin.

In August 2014, John Anthony Walker*, died quietly in a federal prison in Butner, North Carolina. Former Navy Senior Warrant Officer Walker is often called the most notorious

---

* The full story of John A. Walker can be found in a story entitled *The Navy's Biggest Betrayal* detailing his espionage activities and the impact published in the June 2010 issue of the US Naval Institute's Naval History Magazine.

betrayer of U.S naval secrets in history. Walker took advantage of his access to information about weapons and sensor data to pass documents to the Soviet Union, helping it to make significant advances in naval technologies. Without a doubt, Walker's actions constituted one of the most damaging security breaches of the Cold War. Over the 20-year course of his espionage career as an insider with access to some of the US Navy's most sensitive data, Walker passed on over one million pages of secrets. His Soviet handler, Oleg Kalugin, called Walker "by far the most spectacular spy case I handled in the United States."[41] What were Walker's motives? Money and a desire for ego validation.

The Transitional Insider

As the workplace transitioned from a largely paper-based to an increasingly digital environment, so did the insider's *modus operandi*. Larger amounts of data could be extracted by transferring it to removable media such as floppy disks[1*], tapes, or CDs. Or, as the case of Specialist Michael Peri demonstrates, simply by carrying the secrets away on a laptop. In 1989, Peri was a military intelligence analyst assigned to the 11th Armored Cavalry Regiment in Germany. On 20 February, he fled across the West German border into East Germany carrying a laptop computer[*] and military secrets on floppy disks. He returned 15 days later,

---

[*] For those of you born after 1980, a floppy disk is a removable media comprised of a thin magnetic storage medium sealed in a plastic carrier. They were read by a floppy disk drive. Evolving from an 8" down to a 3½" size, floppy disks were the most ubiquitous form of removable data storage from the mid-1970s until the 2000s.

[*] To add a little historical perspective, in 1989 the average laptop weighed about 10-15 pounds and was based on the MS-DOS operating system and applications stored in ROM, had about 20 MB of internal hard disk storage and a slot for 3½" floppy disks that stored about 1.44 MB of data.

stating that he had made a serious mistake. His serious mistake netted him 30 years in Leavenworth, the US military prison.[42] And his motivation? Money.

Bits and Bytes Insider

In recent years, the world has witnessed a continuous parade of insider threat events involving national agencies, industry verticals, and markets. Our environment has become increasing digital, with masses of data able to be moved across the digital boundaries without necessarily relying on the use of the limited storage capabilities of removable media. At the same time, the massive spread of information technology has led to increasing challenges in securing the digital perimeters. Consequently, much of this book addresses the digital insider threat.

Most recently, much of the conversation has centered on the ultimate bits-and-bytes insider, Edward Snowden. Snowden was a systems administrator/analyst working at a regional National Security Agency (NSA) signals intelligence center in Hawaii. He exploited his administrative access to copy millions of megabytes of top secret data before his well-published flight to Hong Kong and then to Moscow. After Snowden's leak, the way government and industry perceived insider threats changed dramatically. His primary motivations – ego and ideology.

CMU SEI has long been a leader in researching the insider threat. In fact, studies date back over 20 years and at least 800 cases involving insider attacks. Signs of employee disgruntlement and escalation of privileges were recurring factors discovered in the CMU SEI studies. Escalation of privileges can be represented as the ability for the potential insider threat to expand on authorized accesses and to assert increased control of the environment or system.

The UK's CPNI conducted its own Insider Data Collection Study, in which the institute analyzed over 120 cases of Insider Threat that took place in the public and private sectors in the UK. The results of their research were consistent with the findings of the CMU SEI and will be incorporated in the discussion of the psychology and demographics of the insider threat.

Edward Snowden was not the first, and he likely won't be the last person to betray his employer – and his nation. So, why has Snowden been called out for an in-depth discussion? When his case is examined through the prism of current research into the characteristics of an insider threat, Snowden demonstrates many of the personality traits and the psychological profile of the insider that has emerged throughout. These profiles are the result of an extensive amount of research to better understand the insider threat and to develop more effective approaches towards detection and defense. Much of this research has been conducted in the US. As early as 1999, RAND* initiated a series of workshops to look at insider threat as a unique problem. For obvious reasons, the US Defense Department also set a series of research initiatives in motion.

Close examination of Snowden may help to answer the following question: Why didn't the National Security Agency, perhaps one of the most technologically

---

* The RAND Corporation is a worldwide organization with its main offices in Santa Monica, California. There are a number of additional locations in the US, the UK, and Belgium. RAND is engaged in numerous research studies geared towards improving policy development and decision making.

sophisticated organizations in the US, detect Snowden's activities? This question, and the answers it receives, are two of the prime reasons for writing this book.

Behavior Traits and Patterns Associated with Insider Threat

Before looking more closely at Snowden as a model case, let's look at some of the most commonly identified patterns of insider threat behaviors. Insider threats may demonstrate a tendency for violating or bypassing organizational rules and regulations. They may have an overly inflated view of their own capabilities, which may evidence itself in bitterness towards those who do not appear to acknowledge their special talents. An insider may tend to perceive criticism or disagreement with supervisors or co-workers as a personal insult that justifies revenge. Some insider threats are impulsive and immature, with little sense of loyalty to anyone or anything.

One word of caution: Just because an individual displays one or more of these behavioral traits does not necessarily mean that they should be judged as untrustworthy or as a potential problem. It does indicate that more attention should be paid to that individual, perhaps even initiating efforts to provide social or psychological assistance. Below is a list of the behavioral characteristics of insider threats, followed by some positive traits that should also be evaluated as a counterbalance that might neutralize the potential to cause damage.

Immaturity/Impulsiveness

Lack of self-control is indicative of an individual with an immature or impulsive personality. These individuals may evolve into insider threats, since they may use poor judgment or be irresponsible and unpredictable. Individuals who are immature or impulsive may also demonstrate a pattern of deceitful, unreliable, or rule-breaking behavior and low self-control.

The insider motivated by impulse may give in to a desire for quick, easy gratification of their financial or emotional desires without considering the full consequences of their actions. Immaturity in an insider threat may be characterized by a propensity towards risk-taking and the belief that one is invincible. Immature individuals want instant gratification rather than achievement of long term goals. Excessive fascination with clandestine espionage and the associated intrigue may be a sign of an immature insider threat.

Risk-seeking is one of the more significant forms of impulsive and immature behavior, particularly when combined with one of the other patterns of behavior. These individuals are restless, cannot resist a dare, and have no tolerance for boredom or lack of activity.

Example: Robert Hanssen

Robert Hanssen[43] was a US Federal Bureau of Investigation (FBI) Special Agent who conducted espionage for the Soviet Union and the Russians for more than 20 years until his 2001 arrest. At work, he appeared quiet and withdrawn, but also occasionally immature and impulsive. As a young man, this was evidenced by several incidents: "During his teenage years, such risks included reckless shooting and irresponsible driving. Once, while shooting at targets in a friend's basement, he suddenly began shooting at the wall as his friends watched in amazement. Frequently, he liked to scare his friends with erratic, fast, and reckless driving."[44]

This apparent lack of self-control continued into Hanssen's adult years, where he engaged in extra-marital sexual encounters and erotic adventures. Evidence appears to indicate that the ventures which led to his selling classified information to the Soviets and the Russians also began as an act of impulse.

As a youth, Hanssen had been fascinated by spy craft. In fact, this fascination led to his choice of a career with the FBI. Once he became an FBI agent, he often announced his plans to "nab Russian spies."[45] When unable to achieve this lofty goal, Hanssen became increasingly disillusioned and displayed disdain for fellow agents who did not appear to share this goal. He also needed money to support an extravagant lifestyle. As a result, he impulsively contacted the KGB* in the early 1990s and began a 20-year career as a spy. For most of these years, Hanssen felt invincible – that his intellectual superiority made him indestructible.

It was this sense of invincibility and superiority that led to his eventual capture and arrest. He began to take ever greater risks, such as hacking into a co-worker's computer to see whether he was being investigated. Despite numerous warning signs, Hanssen remained undetected until 2001, when he was arrested and later sentenced to life in prison.

---

* KGB is the acronym for *Komitet gosudarstvennoy bezopasnosti,* loosely translated as the Committee for State Security. The KGB was the main intelligence agency for the Soviet Union from 1954–1991.

Narcissism

Narcissistic individuals are commonly characterized by feelings of self-importance (perhaps unwarranted), a sense of entitlement, and a lack of empathy for other individuals. At its most extreme is malignant narcissism, which combines common narcissistic behavior with often severe antisocial behaviors.

Narcissistic personalities often grossly overestimate their abilities and exaggerate their accomplishments. They frequently feel that they are entitled to success, power, or admiration – and often need constant reinforcement of their image of themselves. Their need for praise and sensitivity to criticism dominates both their professional and personal relationships. This heightened self-esteem often results in serious doubts and insecurities.

In terms of the insider threat, the narcissistic person often feels that rules made for ordinary individuals do not apply to them. This is accompanied by a sense of entitlement and an unreasonable expectation of privileged treatment. Promotions or rewards should be given simply because they are entitled to them, not necessarily as a result of the quality of their performance. A narcissist may feel justified in punishing their organization or colleagues when their special abilities go unrecognized and unrewarded.

The narcissist views the world only from the perspective of how it affects them. They have little or no ability to empathize with the feelings or needs of others. Indeed, they are often manipulative and have no remorse after using others to achieve their own ends.

Malignant narcissists take these behaviors to an extreme, possibly showing increased aggression towards others, sadism, and a desperate quest for power. This particular brand of narcissist may be especially susceptible to external gratification.

Both the 'standard' and the malignant narcissist may have such a strong need for recognition that, when it is not given, they feel justified in seeking revenge for perceived slights. This becomes a security concern, since this type of insider threat will rationalize their illegal or damaging behaviors by blaming the organization or others. Regret and remorse are not part of their personality make up.

Anti-Social Behavior

Antisocial behavior is often defined as behaviors that habitually defy the commonly accepted rules of society. Antisocial personality disorder may also be known as sociopathy. Manipulation of others and deceitfulness are central characteristics. John Walker, who was used above as an example of narcissism, also epitomizes the antisocial behavior patterns.

Basically, the internal values that would normally inhibit illegal activities are absent. Opportunity to escalate into an insider threat may even be viewed as a justification for action. These individuals enjoy beating the system without getting caught. They may steal, cheat, pick fights, be promiscuous or cruel and abusive.

Antisocial individuals will resent authority and dislike supervision. If they experience a problem at work, they will blame others. They also have an innate ability to manipulate others without remorse.

Example: John Walker

John Anthony Walker, often considered the US's single most damaging spy, is a classic example of both a narcissist and an individual with anti-social behaviors. During his 17-year career, he passed some of the US's most critical secrets to the Soviets and compromised several missions through classified messages and documents he gave to the Soviets. Walker had no remorse about recruiting others to help with his illegal activities, including members of his own family. He used individuals to obtain his own ends and was incapable of empathizing with his own children, who were also arrested and sentenced for their actions in support of Walker's espionage. Robert Hunter, the FBI agent who finally captured Walker, described Walker as one of the most treacherous men he had ever encountered.[46]

Walker was always a somewhat reckless, impulsive individual. As a youth, he damaged property, stole money, and set fires. Later, co-workers would describe him as arrogant and somewhat of a sociopath. He allegedly considered himself a personification of James Bond and spent lavishly on cars, a plane, jewelry, boats, and girlfriends (although married). He frequently boasted about his lavish purchases and had no qualms about lying and doctoring events to suit his desires. Michael Bell, who employed then-retired Walker in his security and investigations company, stated "…I've met murderers, rapists, child molesters. If I had to rank him, Johnny Walker is right up there with them."[47]

After his arrest and sentencing in 1986, Walker showed no remorse for his actions. In fact, he actually appeared to enjoy the exposure. He justified his actions by claiming that they contributed to the end of the Cold War. John Walker has been characterized as a narcissist who rationalized his illegal and damaging activities as normal. Prados summed it up by writing: "He is totally without principle. There was no right or wrong, no morality or immorality, in his eyes. There were only his wants, his own needs, whatever these might be at the moment." In Walker's view, "Everyone is corrupt... everyone has a scam."[48]

Inability to Form a Commitment

Many insider threats exhibit an inability to form and maintain healthy, long term relationships – whether personal or within their organization. These individuals often display a pattern of poor relationships, or an erratic work history including frequent job changes without an accompanying career advancement.

They may have few or no positive work relationships, generally regarding others as less deserving of their attention. Their personal life may be distinguished by a series of broken marriages, unhappy relationships, divorce, and lack of contact with children or family members. This inability to sustain relationships and form commitments is often a result of behaviors that provoke resentment among friends, co-workers and family.

Example: Christopher Boyce

Christopher Boyce and his insider threat activities have been immortalized in the film *The Falcon and the Snowman*, the title of which came from Boyce's love of falcons and his friend Andrew Daulton Lee's drug use issues.

Boyce came from a successful background, but could not commit to either completing his education or remaining in a job. He attended and dropped out of three colleges and left three jobs without giving notice in a very short time span. Over the course of a short and somewhat undistinguished espionage career, Boyce and Lee sold US satellite secrets to the Soviets, but only earned an estimated $77,000.

Vengefulness

A desire for revenge – and perhaps even vindictiveness – is evident in many examples of insider threats. Vindictive behavior can range from physical damage, sabotage of IT systems and networks, to theft of IP or espionage. This type of behavior is often found jointly with narcissism, where the person's self-esteem is based on a grossly inflated opinion of themselves.

Insider threats who act on feelings of revenge are also those who interpret critique, a quarrel, or a failure to recognize their unique capabilities as a personal insult that warrants retribution. They may have unmet expectations – such as not being promoted, being passed over for a salary increase or not getting the high-level projects – that they use as another excuse for revenge.

Paranoia

The last of the behavior patterns to be discussed is paranoia, which may be evidenced in distrust and suspicion of other individuals and their motives. A paranoid insider threat may read hidden meanings into innocent remarks or events, often interpreting these as deliberate.

When paranoia is combined with other signifiers such as revenge or antisocial behavior the paranoid insider threat can be very damaging. This is more likely to occur when the organization, the employer, supervisor or co-worker is viewed as the enemy.

Over-Achievement

One other indicator, which may not be intuitive, is that the insider threat may often appear to be an overly conscientious worker, often volunteering for late shifts or those unwanted work schedules. These over-zealous workers may actually be taking advantage of the absence of observation by others within the organization.

Clearly, not all insider threats demonstrate *all* of these traits, but research has indicated that an unusually large number of insider threat cases possessed at least one or more of the above characteristics. It is also critical to look for mitigating character strengths when considering the behaviors as indicators of possible insider threats. These patterns of character strength include demonstration of a well-developed social consciousness, capacity for loyalty and commitment, sound judgment, and self-discipline.

Insider Motivations and Enablers

Regardless of the nature of the insider activity – sabotage, fraud, industrial or intelligence-related espionage – there are essentially five motivations and enablers: greed, ideology, ego, revenge, and opportunity.

> *"I needed money. Plus, well, I was extremely angry."*
> Former NSA employee and spy David Sheldon Boone, who sold secret information to the Soviet Union from 1988–1991.

Greed

Greed – the desire for earned or unearned financial gain – is one of the most powerful motivators for insider threats. Greed can be driven by a desire for social power – financially-based prestige that comes with expensive automobiles, grand homes, and expensive toys. Classic cases of individuals motivated by greed include Robert Hanssen, Jeffrey Carney, and Aldrich Ames. Greed is linked with personal financial worries, which may cause an individual to turn to fraud, theft, or other espionage for money in an effort to lessen financial pressures.

Ideology

Ideology can be simply defined as a set of beliefs about how the world or a set of behaviors should be. Ideology appears to be the primary motive in several cases involving the theft of sensitive information, particularly from government or military organizations. Patriotism is a form of ideology that may serve as a motive for an individual to become an insider threat. Ideology can be found as a motive for insider threats ranging from environmental rights advocates to a fundamentalist terrorists.

Ego

Greed is a powerful motivator, but the desire for recognition or retribution is at least its equal. Many insiders rationalize that their activities are justified. They are often disgruntled and feel as if they are taken for granted. Perhaps they were passed over for promotion, or have worries about losing their job. Maybe they feel like they do not receive the recognition they deserve or, because they are far down on the organizational ladder, they don't receive all of the incentives – like a new laptop, a company car, or their own administrative assistant.

Revenge

In the study of the insider threat in the UK, the CPNI found that revenge was a primary motivator in less than 10% of cases.[49] At the same time, research indicated that some form of disaffection with the organization was at least a contributing factor in almost all the cases. Insider threat activities with revenge as a motive most often involved acts of sabotage or unauthorized theft of intellectual property or government information. Examples include John Allen Davies and Edwin Earl Pits.

Opportunity

Poor management practices, a weak organizational culture, lack of a strong security foundation – all lead to an environment of opportunity for the hostile insider. CMU SEI MERIT research indicates that lax management controls and the commensurate increased level of opportunity actually lead to an increased tendency to take advantage of the associated freedoms. In fact, research revealed that "lax management encourages escalation of expectation"[50] where already disgruntled employees may try to push the envelope and increase their insider threat behaviors. This appeared to be particularly valid for insiders who already possessed an enhanced sense of entitlement.

Opportunity is most likely to turn into actual insider threat activity when efforts are made to remove or restrict the employee's perceived authorizations or freedom to act.

In looking at the above motivations, both CMU SEI and CPNI came to similar results, as displayed in *Figure 4*.

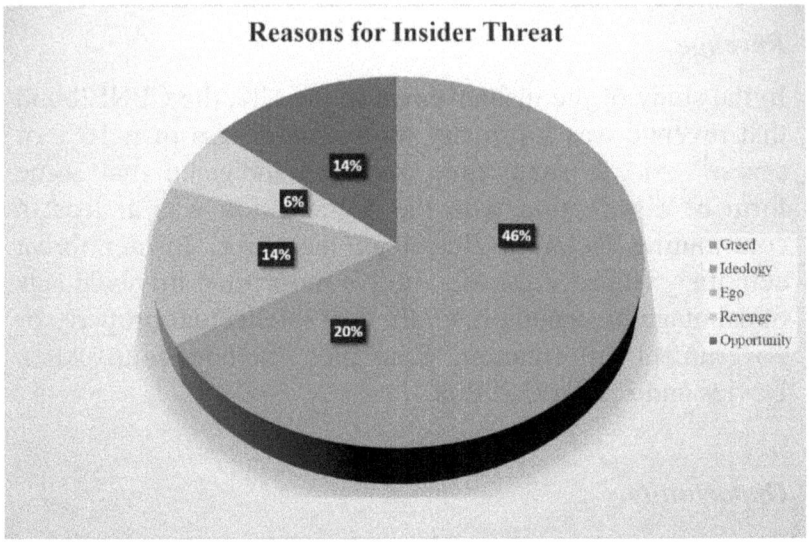

Figure 4: Reasons for insider threat activity (adapted from CMU SEI and CPNI)

The Psychology of an Insider – The Snowden Case

In Snowden's particular case, he appears to have been primarily motivated by a warped sense of entitlement coupled with moral superiority – despite his repeated claims of being on the 'moral high ground' by revealing the activities of the National Security Agency and its so-called intrusions into the lives of US and other nations' citizens.

> "I think there's a little Snowden freak out... There's a million Snowdens of various degrees at work right now, taking data for profit." Bradford Newman, data theft attorney.

According to research conducted by Dr. David L. Charney, almost 90% of the insiders were male and, like Snowden, injury to the male pride and ego appeared to be at the root of many cases of insider threat.[51]

Although Snowden has often been portrayed both by himself and in the media as a lone crusader fighting gallantly against big government's unwarranted intrusion into our personal and professional lives, in reality his personal behavior tells a very different tale – it was a life distinguished by a series of failures, together with his own personal perception that no one really recognized his true abilities. A review of Snowden's case provides an excellent case study in the insider threat, one where many of the personality traits and characteristics were evident – but were, unfortunately, ignored.

Snowden, born in 1983 to a middle-class Coast Guard family, grew into a somewhat rebellious teenager. He failed to graduate from high school, but eventually obtained his GED.* At 17, he entered a local community college where he again fell short of earning a degree. In 2003, Snowden entered the Army Reserve with the goal of becoming a Special Forces soldier. Yet again, he failed; he was dropped from Special Forces training and discharged from the Army a few months after. He took on a new persona, which he called 'The TrueHOOHA', on a gamer and hacker website called Ars Technica*. Under this persona, Snowden

---

* The General Educational Development (GED) refers to a series of four tests that, if passed, provide certification that an individual has US high school level academic skills. Passing this series of exams in science, math, social studies, and reading/writing provides a high school equivalency diploma.
* Ars Technica is a website considered a destination for the community of IT professionals. It was started in 1998 by Ken Fisher and Jon Stokes, and was later sold to Conde Nast in 2008.

addressed his failures by stating online that "great minds do not need a university to make them more credible; they get what they need and quietly blaze their trails into history."

After failing to attain his dream of being a Special Forces soldier, Snowden took a job as a security guard at the University of Maryland Center for the Advanced Study of Language. Somewhere along the line, he jumped from being a university security guard to attaining a position in information technology at the CIA. It was here that he first obtained his Top Secret clearance. While in this job, Snowden bragged online about his hacking skills and landing a position with a national-level intelligence agency without having any formal education or any proven IT skills. He began to demonstrate some of the behaviors that would later lead him to become one of the most notorious insider threats. In fact, the CIA had suspicions that he had attempted to breach classified files, but never provided future employers with any pejorative reports.

It was not until 2009 that Snowden joined the National Security Agency (NSA) – employed first by Dell, and later by the large defense contractor, Booz Allen Hamilton – where he was assigned as a system administrator in Japan and then at a site in Hawaii. Meanwhile, he continued to post his thoughts on the Ars Technica web site. While working as a contractor for the NSA, Snowden underwent a personal transformation. He began to feel he wasn't obtaining the recognition he felt he deserved. He began to blame others for his failings. He became paranoid about being framed by the government. His need for attention grew. He took umbrage at being characterized as a 'low level systems analyst'. But this position as an IT System Administrator provided Snowden with the perfect cover for accessing classified files. He frequently volunteered to work the late or holiday shifts, thus ensuring that he would be largely unobserved.

Over time, Snowden increasingly began to embody the narcissistic ideal, and inflated egoism led him to justify his actions to himself with the thought that he was actually safeguarding democracy through his actions. As in most of his other activities, Snowden just didn't fit in. His unpleasant personality alienated many of his co-workers.[52] They viewed him as reticent, he described himself as an ascetic. During his NSA employment, he realized that the Hawaii facility did not have the audits sufficient to trace his unauthorized access to millions of classified computer files. Snowden made the decision that it was his calling to expose the NSA's surveillance programs and that his decision to steal and reveal thousands of highly classified documents and operations was based solely upon his desire "to improve NSA."*

The initial damage assessment estimated that Snowden downloaded about 1.7 million documents, of which approximately 1% have been released as of the time of writing. The damage assessment of Snowden's insider activities recorded massive fallout for US foreign relations, undercover operations worldwide were compromised, and thousands of man hours and millions of dollars have been spent in attempts to reconstruct all the files Snowden may have taken.

Ego and the sense of entitlement can allow the insider to rationalize the crime they are committing. Add to that unrestricted privileged access to system resources enjoyed by Snowden – and you have the perfect storm.

---

* Stated in a December 2013 interview with the *Washington Post.*

Employees and contractors such as Snowden, with vast privileged access to the information system and the sensitive data it contains, present a serious risk of intentionally, accidentally, or indirectly misusing that privilege access and stealing, deleting, or modifying data. Human nature remains the weakest link when it comes to the juncture of people, process, and technology — the three basic tenets of a security program — and Edward Snowden is a perfect example.

While many of the known insiders examined in the research by CMU SEI and the CPNI exhibit one or more of the behaviors, the Snowden case is unique in that each of the traits illustrated in *Figure 5* below were clearly visible, if only his managers and co-workers had taken the time to recognize them.[53]

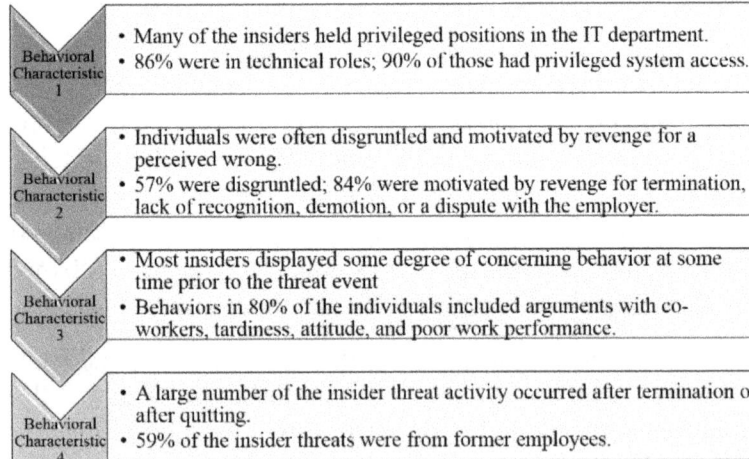

Figure 5: Insider threat behavior characteristics (adapted from research findings from the CMU SEI)

Organizational Characteristics and Insider Threat

When looking at insider threat models and indicators, the culture of the organization and its characteristics cannot be ignored as having a role, particularly in providing either motivation or opportunity for an insider threat to act.

Many of these characteristics were consistent across organizations that have been victims of insider threat activity. In fact, they could also be considered traits that enable the insider to act. These characteristics are presented here; best practices to mitigate the traits are detailed in *Chapter 6*.

Poor Management Practices

Poor management practices most often manifest in an absence of supervision or direct oversight of employee activity. As a result, many of the personality traits, behaviors, and insider activities were either unnoticed or not addressed.

Lack of Sufficient Auditing

Those organizations that neglected their auditing, whether of practices or the use of their IT systems, were less able to be in a position to quickly identify irregularities or unusual behaviors. Insider threat activities went without detection, or went undetected for much longer than necessary.

Ineffective or Non-Enforced Security Controls

Organizations may have chosen security controls that were insufficient in addressing their true security needs, or did not enforce those they had implemented. Some of the most common deficiencies involved the non-application of 'need to know' and lack of separation of duties and least privilege. These practices allowed insiders more access than required, or put them in a position of elevated trust where they could manipulate the systems without oversight.

Absence of a Culture of Security

A poor security culture is often evidenced by a general disregard for security practices and a failure to take positive action when security practices are violated. Effective security training and positive reinforcement of the organization's security goals are two of the elements most often lacking in organizations that have a poor security culture.

Limited or Absent re- and Post-Employment Employee Screenings

While many organizations conduct pre-employment employee screenings, these may be limited in scope. The limitations may be a result of legal restraints, lack of access to appropriate screening resources, or limited experience on the part of the screeners. In addition, the detail of the screenings may not be commensurate with the sensitivity or access allowed by the position.

Additionally, once an individual passes the initial screening and is employed by the organization, post-employment screenings either do not take place or they occur at intervals that might be too long to enable insider threat detection.

Finally, contracted personnel, consultants or partner individuals are rarely screened by the organization they are indirectly supporting. A great deal of faith is placed in the providing organization, with the assumption that due diligence is being exercised in its pre- and post-employment screening practices.

No Shared Communication between Organizational Elements

Studies have indicated that, while one part of an organization may have been concerned about a potential insider threat behavior, this concern was not consistently shared across the organization. The UK CPNI study on insider threat activity clearly revealed that: "If an organization does not communicate and share information about threats and risks, but keeps the information in organizational silos, then its ability to mitigate insider activity is severely reduced."[54]

Insider threat activity would be less likely if information about performance and employee welfare issues held by the Human Resources department, knowledge by the security staff of attempts at breaches of the physical security, or incidents of IT violations, were shared across all of these organizational elements.

Lack of Executive Engagement

Employees tend to emulate the practices of their senior management. If supervisors, managers, and executives respect and comply with security practices, the employees are also more likely to do so. A lack of executive engagement and unclear management direction can increase the likelihood that insider threat activity will occur.

Good management and supervisory security practices are more likely to engender a responsible work force, minimize feelings of discontent, and ensure that all employees and other individuals know that counter-productive behaviors will be quickly identified and consistently addressed.

The Life Stages of the Insider Threat

Dr. David L. Charney in his studies into the psychology of the insider spy identified that insider threat development appears to be a dynamic evolution and not a static personality state. He talked of it in terms of the "movie of a person's life… and as the movie unfolds, things happen to the main character, some good and some bad. Drama gets added when adversities, stress, challenges, and disappointments pile up in excess. Some of these adverse events are due to poor personal choices."[55]

Although Charney was focused on the insider spy, the 10 Stages he identified may fit equally well for any other type of insider threat. *Figure 6* depicts the stages identified in Charney's research.

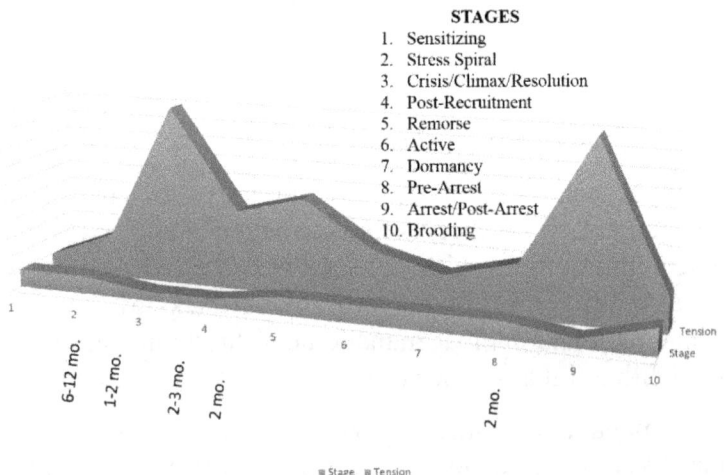

STAGES
1. Sensitizing
2. Stress Spiral
3. Crisis/Climax/Resolution
4. Post-Recruitment
5. Remorse
6. Active
7. Dormancy
8. Pre-Arrest
9. Arrest/Post-Arrest
10. Brooding

Figure 6: 10 Stages of the insider

Let's examine these in more detail, as they provide valuable insight into the insider.

Stage 1: Sensitizing

The negative experiences we have throughout childhood, adolescence, and adulthood may scar and sensitize us, or they may create an ambition to be stronger, smarter, and more successful. As we progress through life, the so-called hard knocks caused by financial problems, health issues, or being passed over for promotion may tip an individual over the line, creating "a psychological perfect storm."[56]

Stage 2: Stress/Spiral

Life is rarely fair; on the contrary, it is filled with inequities and injustices. For some, very little seems to go right – they don't get that promotion, they experience a financial setback, or they may simply feel that their true potential is not recognized. While some may rise above these setbacks, for others these challenges may cause a stress spiral that puts them on the decision path to become an insider threat.

Stage 3: Crisis/Climax/Resolution

According to Dr. Charney, those in Stage 3 may choose to direct their energies outward and take action against others. They have "an intolerable sense of personal failure as privately defined by that person" and "they will need to deny their sense of inner failure and prefer to blame and project their inner sense of badness outwardly onto others."[57] This is the stage where an individual may become abusive towards loved ones or he could "go postal."* Those that become insider threats may "self-recruit" as they see malicious insider activity as a means to take revenge on those individuals or organizations they view as having done them wrong.

Stage 4: Post-Recruitment

In this stage, the insider has fully validated his/her actions and feels a sense of justification – or even elation – at their self-recruitment. This phase may last for quite a while, as the insider sees their actions as positive and has an increased sense of self-worth.

Stage 5: Morning After Remorse

Although some insiders may never reach this stage, there are others that may begin to reflect and have doubts about the actions taken while in the euphoric post-recruitment phase. There may be a sense of being trapped and unable to undo what has been done. Suddenly, their actions seem to take on a life of their own.

Stage 6: Active Insider Stage

At this stage, the insider begins to accept that they are no longer able to undo their actions and may even progress to a state where they again feel justified in their activities. At

---

* The term 'go postal' means to fly into a violent rage, often provoked by workplace stress. It originated in the US in the mid-1980s, when several US postal workers shot and killed other postal workers and innocent bystanders. According to The Phrase Finder, it was first used by a writer for the Petersburg Times in December 1993. (Source: *www.phrases.org.uk/meanings/159050.html*)

the same time, the insider may have doubts about their survival or ability to evade eventual punishment. It's now only a matter of time until they are made to pay, and some may even subconsciously hope for detection and the final penalty for their actions.

Stage 7: Dormancy

The insider may grow tired of the fear and now goes to ground. The once-brilliant solution devised by the insider now becomes a nightmare. The insider tries to run away or hide, or simply becomes inactive.

Stage 8: Pre-Detection and Punishment (Pre-Arrest)

The insider may begin to notice signs that their activity has been detected and that there will be consequences. Dr. Charney called this stage "pre-arrest," but it may be the stage where any form of impending punishment threatens the insider. Feeling a sense of impending doom, the insider may become careless or even take actions to precipitate their own punishment.

Stage 9: Punishment and Post-Punishment (Arrest and Post-Arrest)

It's over; the insider is caught and appropriately punished. Still, most insiders tend to display no sense of remorse. A final disappointment is added to the insider's existing sense of failure, or the insider may revert to something like Stage 3, where they see themselves as a hero. John Walker Jr., often described as running the most damaging spy ring in our nation's history, showed no remorse during the long years of his prison sentence. In fact, he continued to be proud of how he had duped the US intelligence community during the decades of his active spy career. Edward Snowden declared that he "has no regrets about spilling some of America's most closely kept secrets and said he sees himself as a patriot trying to do right."[58]

Stage 10: Brooding

Time goes by and notoriety and fame have passed. The insider loses some of his/her sense of justification and superiority. The insider may go quiet, become more contemplative, or even go so far as to provide advice on how to protect an organization or a nation from someone like him/herself.

The Radicalized Insider Threat

The US Department of the Army (DA) also identified a "Radicalization Process" while searching for a way to identify insider threats that might later evolve into terrorists.[59] The process has been adapted in *Figure 7* from a focus to instead cover possible indicators of an evolution of other types of insider threat behaviors. The main difference between this model and Charney's model is that it focuses on four steps leading up to the insider threat activity. Charney's model takes the insider threat beyond the action phase to results that can occur after insider threat activity.

The DA model illustrates an evolutionary process, where the insider threat evolves from a pre-threat to action. In the pre-threat phase, the insider begins to develop a rationale for the insider threat activity he/she is contemplating. This can involve a perceived lack of recognition, failure to be promoted, or – in the case of the insider terrorist – an increasing radicalization.

From here, the insider becomes increasingly disgruntled or radicalized and the justification for the insider threat event becomes more concrete in his or her mind. This moves the insider seamlessly to the justification phase, where the insider becomes convinced that 'they deserve what they get'.

The final evolutionary phase is where the insider actively engages in their threat activity. This phase can be short – a single threat event – or it can be long, as in the case of John Walker, who operated as an insider over two decades.

The Evolution of an Insider Threat			
PRE-THREAT	**MOTIVATION**	**JUSTIFICATION**	**ACTION**
Motivation/ Conversion	Individual justifies actions	Individual is convinced action is required for a specific cause.	Individual knowingly engages in Insider Threat activity
• Jilted Believer – Increased Bitterness	• "My value is not recognized"	• Rationale strengthened	• Facilitation
• Acceptance Seeker	• Increased isolation from former life and/or co-workers	• Identity strengthened	• Preparation
• Conversion			• Financing
• Behavioral Changes	• Development of new social identity	• Increased training	• Planning
• Self-Promotion		• Target Surveillance	• Execution
• Other	Key Components		
Opportunity	• Disgruntlement		
• Access	• Ideological changes		
• Employment			
Motivation Development	Acceptance	Conviction	Insider Threat Act
No Action	Propensity for Action	Ready for Action	**Action**

Figure 7: Evolution of an insider threat

Demographics and the Insider Threat

Interestingly, both the CMU SEI, the CPNI, and Dr. Charney's research have found fairly consistent demographic characteristics among the studied insider threats. One of these is that most of the malicious insider activities are conducted by men. CPNI found that 82% of insider threats were male and only 18% were female.[60] Dr. Charney postulates that this may be the result of the different value systems of men and women: historically, men value career success while women may have a more holistic sense of what constitutes success.

Some of the other noteworthy demographic observations include:

- Approximately half of the insider threat activities were conducted by individuals between the ages of 30 and 45 years old.
- The majority of insider activity was executed by permanent employees of the organization; less than 10% were contractor or temporary staff.
- Insiders were almost evenly split between administrative staff and lower and mid-level managerial staff. There were a relatively small number of cases involving executive level staff.
- More than half of the insider threat activity occurred between the 1st and 5th years of employment.

A Note of Caution – Privacy and Ethical Concerns

This chapter provided insight into a number of personal and organizational characteristics that could predict a potential for insider threat. However, there is an "inherent tension between an organization safeguarding its assets and employee privacy rights."[61]

There have been several legal cases that have firmly established an organization's legal right to monitor their employees or have access to personal information. Work-related activity may be legally monitored in order to identify and correct inappropriate or suspicious behavior. However, it's important to remember that mutual trust is a fundamental concept underlying employee/organizational relationships. The perception that an organization may be overly extending its monitoring activities or use of personal information can easily create an environment of negativity and mutual distrust.

Organizations must walk a fine line between an individual's expectation of privacy and the organization's right to self-protection. While the insider threat is very real, most organizations consist of a high percentage of staff that are honest, hardworking individuals who could be offended by the perception that they are being overly scrutinized by their employer. The individual without guilt will quickly resent the sensation of being 'guilty until proven innocent', and there is also a risk of incurring damage to the organization or the individual as a result of false accusations.

The knowledge of monitoring itself can result in increased stress, lower productivity, and higher levels of discontent among the employees. Monitoring perceived as invasive – with an implied lack of trust – can actually contribute to an employee's dissatisfaction, and excessive management intervention in suspected issues may actually increase the potential for an insider threat to emerge. The use of personal information, such a medical records and knowledge of personal life events, for threat detection may not be appropriate or legal.

At the same time, one successful case of insider threat sabotage or information theft could result in a great deal of damage and cost – both financial and reputational. To an organization, this risk may "warrant monitoring all behavioral and demographic employee data available to prevent incidents."[62] Personal life events can be predictors of increased stress and may push an individual into engaging in damaging behaviors. In fact, research also indicates that lack of attention and organizational engagement may actually increase insider activity. Trying to find this balance between respect for individual privacy and protection of the organization has been described as a "trust trap."[63]

In order to avoid this trap and to ensure employee understanding of the monitoring process and requirements, the organization must ensure that all monitoring practices are fully disclosed, clarified, and managed fairly across the entire organization. Since privacy protection laws vary widely between nations, or even between US states, every organization must ensure that they are fully aware of the restrictions. If necessary, legal counsel should be sought prior to establishing any monitoring program.

Recommendations for Additional Reading
Pete Earley. *Family of Spies: Insider the John Walker Spy Ring*. Bantam Publishing. November 1988.
Privacy Rights Clearinghouse. Fact Sheet 7: Workplace Privacy and Employee Monitoring. *www.privacyrights.org/ workplace-privacy-and-employee-monitoring*

CHAPTER 3: THE UNINTENTIONAL INSIDER THREAT

A lot of evil in the world is actually not intentional.
– *George Soros[64]

One of the greatest concerns is that 'good' employees can accidentally jeopardize security through unintentional data leaks or other errors. Some of these employees may be victims of social engineering; others may be unintentionally exposing themselves or their employer's data through the use of social media.

Throughout the earlier chapters of this book, the focus has been on intentional insiders, who receive much of the insider threat 'hype'. These are individuals who plan to cause damage. However, not all insider threats are deliberate. There is someone else who can endanger an organization – let's call them the unintentional insider threat (UIT). As Christopher Young, Vice President at RSA, has pointed out, these types of incidents may not be as 'sexy' as the splashy stories of malicious fraud conducted by disgruntled employees, but they are imminently more problematic to enterprises.[65]

The UIT could be anyone inside an organization – the co-worker sitting down the hall, your supervisor, the administrative assistant to the CEO, or anyone else. Without considering the consequences, they may leave sensitive documents out in plain view, share passwords,

---

* George Soros is a prominent investor, known for his stock trades. He is also called 'The Man Who Broke the Bank of England', because of a destructive US $10 billion short sale.

bypass established security procedures or transfer corporate IP to the Cloud without approval.

So, who is the UIT? It's a person who, through human error or inattention, can unknowingly compromise or cause damage to their organization. This could be anyone – even you!

The CMU SEI research team has proposed the following working definition of the unintentional insider threat: "An unintentional insider threat is (1) a current or former employee, contractor, or business partner (2) who has or had authorized access to an organization's network, system, or data and who, through (3) their action/inaction without malicious intent, (4) negatively affects the confidentiality, integrity, or availability of the organization's information or information systems."[66] While this definition is clearly focused on the unintentional insider threat to IT, it can be expanded to include the physical aspects of an organization as well.

However, Carnegie Mellon's David Mundie's research studies into the unintentional insider threat indicate that the unintentional and the intentional insider threat share a number of features. The common feature for both types of insider threat appears to be a lack of a security culture and secure management practices, which increase the likelihood of human error on the part of the UIT and also provide increased opportunity for the intentional insider threat.

There is no doubt that UIT incidents should be considered equally important to intentional threats. The realms of business and government are replete with unintentional acts that have resulted in large financial or reputational losses. The unintentional insider may actually pose a greater threat to an organization than the intentional insider.

What makes the UIT so dangerous? There are a number of reasons:

- Numbers – there may be only one intentional insider threat within an organization, but there might be tens or even hundreds of UITs.

- Misperception of actions – the UIT may actually think they are performing their job correctly or playing by the rules, but in fact they may actually be violating a policy or accessing information for which they have no authorization. Telework or the use of mobile devices only increases this problem.

- Susceptibility – a capable social engineer, whether within or external to the same organization, can take advantage of the UIT in order to gain access or information.

- Detectability – the UIT does not usually demonstrate detectable behaviors that would highlight the possibility of a potential threat. Their actions do not correspond with the intentional insider threat behavioral analysis models that are being developed, because there is no malicious intent to detect.

There are many ways in which an employee can become a UIT. Most are the victims of social engineering, which is a form of external manipulation of the insider in order to illegally obtain sensitive information. This is the naïve, but unintentional insider.

There are also cases of employees who find a thumb drive and plug it into their work computer. Once the drive is inserted, it installs malware that leads to the compromise of the corporate network.

Let's discuss some of the ways an employee can become a UIT.

Social Engineering

Social engineering can be loosely defined as the "manipulation of people to get them to unwittingly perform actions that cause harm (or increase the probability of causing future harm) to the confidentiality, integrity or availability of the organization's resources or assets, including information, information systems, or financial systems."[67]

Malicious social engineering activities can involve either direct communications (in person or via phone) or indirect exchanges such as email. Successful social engineering attacks capitalize on an understanding of the weakness of the human psyche and are often based on people skills such as sympathy, friendliness, impersonation, or other methods to establish a trust relationship and gain desired access or information.

Phishing, Pharming, Vishing and SMiShing!

Phishing, Pharming, Vishing, and SMiShing are all indirect forms of social engineering used to take advantage of the UIT. Phishing is essentially a malicious activity designed to trick individuals into a desired action through unauthorized methods. Phishers can infect computers with malware or convince individuals to participate unwittingly in activities that can damage their organization.

Most phishing activities are associated with spoofed emails that look authentic and mimic banks, credit card companies or other businesses. Initial phishing efforts were often simple and fraught with spelling and grammatical errors, but the new phishers have become increasingly sophisticated. They often use real company logos and legitimate-looking emails that replace real links with ones that direct a victim to a fraudulent web page. Most of the messages in the emails prompt the intended victim to take a specific action, for example by threatening to cancel an account if the individual does not reply swiftly.

EXAMPLE OF A PHISHING EMAIL

Subject: Upgrade Your Account
Date: November 20, 2015

Your mailbox john.smith@business.com has exceeded its storage limits set by your email Administrator. You will not be able to receive any new email until you revalidate your account.

Click on the link <badlink> and login with your current account information to revalidate your Account.

Webmail Help Desk Administrator

Figure 8: Example of a phishing email

In most methods, emails to company employees appear to be an official communication that requires the recipient to click on an embedded link – which then takes them to the fake site – or asks them to open an attachment, which infects the machine with malware. Phishing emails may masquerade as communications from a government agency, a business partner, the internal IT staff, or from a company executive.

Once on a fake site, the employee may be asked to perform some actions, such as to log in with their credentials. The attacker is then able to capture and use the employee's information. Although there are many kinds of phishing, attachments may well indicate that "… the largest threat is the possibility that malware is delivered into the corporate environment."[68] In addition to the 'generic' form of phishing, there are other related types of attacks: Spear phishing, which targets particular individuals or companies; and whaling, which focuses on the organization's executives. In many organizations today, "top-ranking management personnel are older and less technology-savvy than the new hires of the very same organization... these managers have more responsibility and access to resources, yet likely have less technical expertise or training."[69]

Pharming is another type of scam. It is similar to phishing in that it uses bogus websites. While phishing entices a user to click on a phony link or attachment, pharming actually re-directs the individual to a bogus site even if the user has entered a correct website URL.* A further enhancement is 'drive by' pharming, in which the DNS settings on a broadband router or wireless access point are changed, redirecting the user to a fraudulent web site, such as a copy of a bank web page, without their knowledge. Symantec researcher Zulfikar Ramzan explained how this works: "Whenever you'd want to go to the bank site, instead of the real one, you'd get the attacker's fake site. The danger is that this drive-by pharming attack is so silent and there's only subtle telltale signs that it's occurring."[70]

Vishing, or voice phishing, is the phone version of phishing. This form of phishing relies heavily on social engineering to trick an individual into revealing information that can be used for unauthorized access to online accounts or other online areas. In vishing scams, the target individual will receive a call on their home or mobile phone pretending to be from a trusted source, such as a bank. Recently, the US Better Business Bureau (BBB) alerted

---

* URL stands for Uniform Resource Locator, which is a unique address or specific path to a site on the Internet. Its function is similar to a street address.

consumers to a vishing scam in which a caller, usually with an Indian accent, claims to be from Microsoft. Claiming that problems have been identified with the user's Microsoft product, the person offers to solve the computer problem, but the real goal is to gain unauthorized access to the consumer's information system. In fact, the author of this book received several phone calls from a man identifying himself as being from Microsoft tech support. The calls ceased immediately when the caller was told that his scam was recognized and would be reported to the US FCC.*

SMiShing, short for SMS phishing, uses cell phone text messages to lure the unintentional insider into following a link or responding to a message. In most cases, a SMiShing text will come from a '5000' number, which indicates that the source is an email and not another mobile phone. McAfee Labs identified one SMiShing scam that sent text messages telling the recipients that they will be charged for a service unless they access a link to cancel the order. If they did so, a malicious code would be downloaded that would turn their device into a zombie on a bot network*.

Some of these malicious activities used a mix of the above tactics. The Internet Patrol and Nextgov's ThreatWatch (*www.nextgov.com/cybersecurity/threatwatch/2015/02/breach/2016/*) warned in February 2015 about a scam integrating phishing, vishing and SMiShing, which directed account holders from Bank of America, Wells Fargo, and Key Bank

---

* The US Federal Communications Commission regulates communications by radio, television, wire, satellite, and cable in the US. The FCC also maintains a communications fraud database and will take action on reported threats.
* Norton (*http://us.norton.com/botnet/*) defines a botnet as a network of infected information systems made up of infected machines known as zombies or bots.

to call a hijacked Holiday Inn phone number. A call to the phone number played a recorded message prompting the caller to enter their credit/debit card number.

Subterfuge is the use of deception to achieve a specific goal. While this may include phishing, it may also involve social engineering to mislead individuals into revealing account information, or misdirecting individuals to counterfeit sites. For example, the attacker may establish a fake web site that imitates a bank associated with the target organization.

The Careless UIT

Then there is the careless UIT. These individuals may take actions that endanger their organization by intentionally or unintentionally bypassing official procedures, as they justify doing so by saying to themselves that they just want to get the job done for the good of the company. The careless UIT may expose the company to harm despite their best intentions.

Organizations today are often so intent on identifying the intentional insider threat that they overlook the fact that data leakage as a result of carelessness may be taking place right under their noses. Much of this careless data leakage today takes place via social media postings.

Social Media and the UIT

The increased adoption of mobile technologies, such as smart phones, the Bring Your Own Device (BYOD) to work movement, and the rise in the use of social media at home and at the office have blurred the separation between work and personal life. This evolution requires organizations to re-evaluate their security boundaries in order to implement appropriate precautionary measures. When personally-owned devices and social media are available at work locations, significant issues regarding security responsibility appear. Overall responsibility for detecting and preventing security incidents, such as malware on mobile devices or the posting of sensitive or classified information to social media sites, is often ill-defined. Implementing appropriate security policies and procedures is rendered more difficult when organizations also have to consider the boundaries between individual rights and organizational needs.

One of the primary underlying challenges is "that those responsible for the defense of ICT systems and data tend to be of a generation with characteristic attributes at odds with those performing the essential roles of the day to day business and government. The different generational mind sets hold divergent ideals of loyalty and work ethic."[71]

In his research on social media and the insider threat, Colin Armstrong refers to the TPP Triangle – or Technology, Process and People. Of these three, the People leg of the triangle is the most difficult to address. In recent years, organizations have accepted – and often even welcomed – the idea of a more temporary workforce that can be ramped up or down as required by organizational needs. Unlike the Baby Boomers, who still possessed remnants of the sense of loyalty to employers common in the previous generation, members of the new Generation Y and Millennials are not only more technically literate, "they are also continually connected via social media applications ... do not distinguish between work and their private lives, and importantly maintain a loyalty to self to the exclusion of others."[72]

Additionally, these generations have a culture of sharing, where it may be difficult for them to recognize appropriate boundaries between information that can be shared and information that should not be exposed outside of their organization. The loyalty primarily to self, together with a sharing culture, may lead to a UIT.

This phenomenon requires private and public sector organizations to adjust their current security procedures. Most existing security programs assume a certain level of loyalty to the organization, but this assumption may no longer hold true and should not form the basis for the establishment of an effective security program. Resolving these security challenges will require a more multi-layered approach to risk and risk management and may require the deployment of more sophisticated process and technology tools.

Recommendations for Additional Reading
Phishing Quiz 2.0 – Can you spot a phish? *https://blog.opendns.com/2011/11/30/phishing-quiz-v2-0-can-you-spot-a-phish/*

CHAPTER 4: INSIDER THREAT, BIG DATA AND THE CLOUD

The cloud computing model may be a wonderful system when it works; a nightmare when it fails.
– *Jamais Cascio[73]

Data protection in general, and in particular protection against the insider, has been rendered more difficult by technologies such as the Cloud and big data.

Increasingly, governmental and private organizations move toward consolidation of their information technology resources. In many cases, this means centralization, the dissolving of corporate-owned boundaries, the movement of data into the Cloud, and the evolution of 'big data'. It doesn't take long to understand that this consolidation of information leads to a higher target density – one of infinitely higher value to an insider theat. The old adage 'trust no one' may be particularly relevant to today's information and Cloud-driven organizations. The fundamental nature of the insider threat is not changed by the Cloud, but the Cloud environment does allow for new threat opportunities.

Cloud Computing

Before a discussion of the threats to the Cloud, it is important to gain a clearer understand of Cloud computing

---

* Jamais Cascio is best known as a futurist who writes extensively about emerging technologies and future scenarios.

in general. Cloud computing streamlines access to data – but the move to virtualization and the Cloud increases the risk and dangers posed by an insider. The term "Cloud computing" is everywhere, but what is the Cloud? Where is the Cloud? Are we even in the Cloud?

In simple terms, Cloud computing is defined as the shared storage of, and access to, data and programs over the web, rather than through local servers or personal computers. The word "Cloud" is used as a metaphor for the web; different services – such as data storage and applications – are 'float above' the organization and are delivered to its users through the internet.

Imagine that you are a large corporation. All of your employees need the right hardware, software, and data storage in order to do their jobs. Not only do you have to furnish computers for everyone, you also have to purchase software and licenses. And not just once – you need to ensure patching and upgrades as hardware and software change. To manage all of these users and their data, you purchase servers, backup storage, and networking tools. Every day you look at the huge amount of resources you need just to manage this ever-growing and changing environment. But now, with Cloud computing, remote systems owned by a virtualization company run everything from email to word processing and complex data analysis applications.

The Cloud allows for a significant shift of the workload from the local organization to a central, virtualized environment. The large, amorphous network of computers that make up a part of the Cloud takes care of everything. The only thing the users now require is the interface software, which can be as simple as a web browser and the

Cloud takes care of the rest. The Cloud provides significant advantages in terms of scalability, flexibility and services that cannot be obtained as easily in a localized data center environment. In 2015, Vormetric released its *Global Report on Insider Threat*[74], which indicated that the top three locations where data is at risk are corporate databases (49%), file servers (39%), and the Cloud (36%). The threat percentage of the Cloud is likely to rise as its rapid growth continues.

Before we can address Cloud computing concerns, let's try to understand Cloud services and deployment models. There are essentially three types of Cloud services (SaaS, PaaS, and IaaS) and three deployment models (private, public, and hybrid). *Figure 9* shows the relationship of the three Cloud service deployment models.

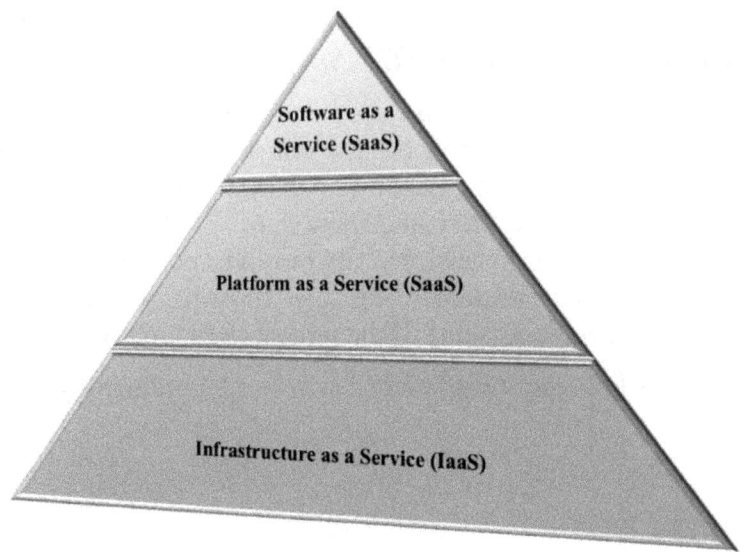

Figure 9: Cloud service models

Software as a Service (SaaS)

SaaS provides access to online software solutions. The SaaS provider has total control of the application. Examples include social media platforms and Customer Relationship Management Software (CRMS).

Platform as a Service (PaaS)

The PaaS model provides a pre-built application platform to a client, so the clients do not have to build an underlying infrastructure for their necessary applications. On the backend a PaaS provider automatically scales and provisions the required infrastructure elements based on application requirements. Amazon Web Services is an example of a PaaS provider.

Infrastructure as a Service (IaaS)

In the IaaS model, the IaaS provider supports not only the applications for the client, but the entire data infrastructure. This includes virtual machines, storage, firewalls, load balancers, and more. Here, the clients not only have access to the applications they need, but also to the operating system, the management dashboard of the firewall, or the load balancer. Terremark is one of the largest IaaS providers.

Now let's talk about the various types of Cloud deployment models.

Private Cloud

Private Cloud is implemented, deployed, and managed within a single organization.

Public Cloud

A Public Cloud is comprised of a set of resources provided by a third-party organization such as Amazon Web Services or Google AppEngine.

Hybrid Cloud

The hybrid Cloud is a mix of private and public Clouds.

Figure 10 illustrates some of the primary characteristics of the Cloud deployment models.

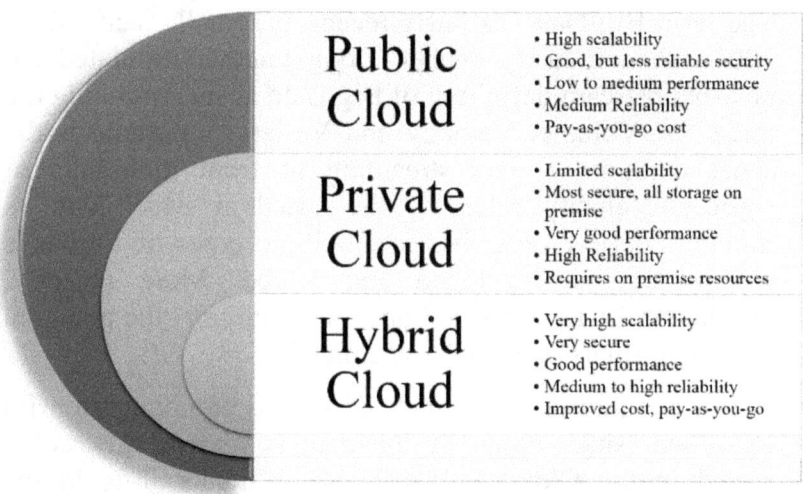

Figure 10: Cloud deployment models

Big Data

Wikipedia defines Big Data as "data sets so large or complex that traditional data processing applications are inadequate." Oxford Dictionaries provides some additional context, defining Big Data as "extremely large data sets that must be analyzed computationally to reveal patterns, trends, and associations." Big Data is constantly being generated by every digital process, social media exchanges, sensors, mobile devices, and other sources. It is arriving from these various sources at an alarming rate of velocity, volume, and variety. One commonly accepted fact is that Big Data needs equally 'big protection'.

The term Big Data" is fairly recent. It actually stems from 2001, when industry analyst Doug Laney formulated the now-mainstream definition of Big Data as incorporating the three Vs: Volume, Velocity and Variety.[75] Volume is the sheer amount of data streaming in from thousands of sources. Velocity refers to the speed at which data is moving. Variety describes the multiple types of format is which data is developed and stored. More recently, 'Variability' was added to Laney's definition – the potential for data formats to change dynamically.

Cloud computing is often discussed in combination with Big Data, since much of the data is increasingly being stored in the Cloud infrastructure. Whether it is in the Cloud or on their own networks, organizations are collecting and electronically storing enormous amounts of information.

Big Data's weakness lies in the unprecedented aggregation of data, when data is gathered together like this, it represents a concentrated, high-value target to adversaries. As Big Data becomes more ubiquitous, this problem only gets worse. Big Data magnifies the threats that insiders can pose, largely because one insider may be able to access a great deal of sensitive or classified information.

Big Data's value is that organizations can use it to detect trends and patterns, which can drive improved business and mission results. Consequently, while the large data sets common to Big Data can be a tempting target for hackers and cyber criminals, Big Data can also be used to assist in insider threat detection. Several companies have developed Big Data analytical tools that combine real-time correlation and anomaly detection to widen insider threat detection. One of the Big Data solutions being explored by the US DoD is the continuous evaluation of personnel by correlating multiple data sources to create an individual profile. In 2014, James Clapper, Director of National Intelligence (DNI), expressed his support for the use of Big Data to assist the US Government in anticipating insider threat behavior.[76]

Cloud Computing & Big Data Insider Threat Concerns

Although a relatively recent technology, it is a rare IT conversation today that does *not* include reference to the Cloud. Government agencies and companies alike are using the power of Cloud computing as a key operations enabler. In fact, the US implemented a "Cloud First" mandate in 2011, requiring Federal agencies to evaluate and implement Cloud-based technologies before considering an investment in local network centers. The UK is also promoting its version of Cloud mandate, called the G-Cloud framework.[77]

Cloud Security Concerns

At a time when so much has gone mobile, where social networking is redefining interpersonal and business communications, organizations view the Cloud as an opportunity to reimagine their business model. Virtualization* and Cloud technologies offer great benefits – they provide simple, one-stop access to applications, data, and other networking tools without the organization having to own and maintain the infrastructure.

At the same time, trust is a big concern for businesses using Cloud services. The very idea of handing over the 'crown jewels' to another company causes many executives more than a few worry lines. Cloud services have magnified the potential consequences of intentional insider threat or unintentional user error by facilitating the movement of large amounts of data into and out of the enterprise. *Figure 11* illustrates the primary concerns that executives have around the loss of sensitive information – the Cloud is at the top of the list.

---

* Virtualization is a type of software that allows multiple operating systems to run simultaneously on a single physical machine, thus saving time, money, and space. The benefit of virtualization is that it allows an increase in the scale of the information system infrastructure without having to add additional physical hardware, thereby reducing 'server creep' and allows computing resources to be used more efficiently.

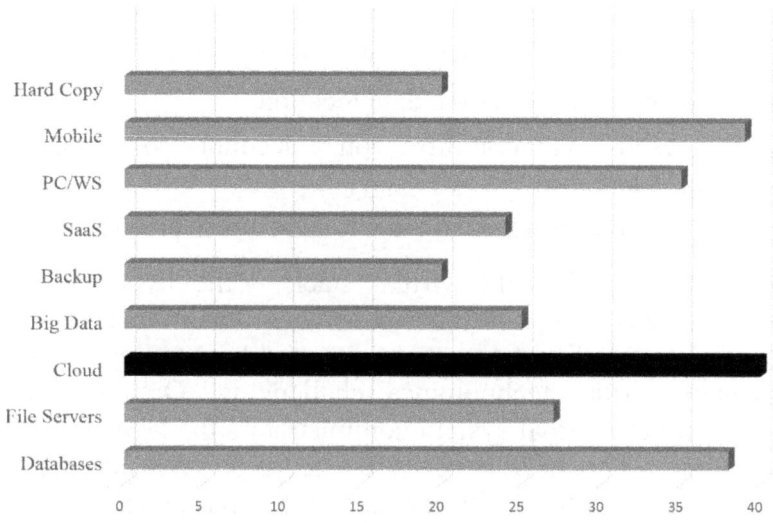

**Figure 11: Perception of risk for various data
environments**

Concerns range from questions about the ownership of the
data to availability of data when needed and the security
and privacy of the information. Exfiltration of corporate
data to the Cloud is, in reality, a low technology
undertaking, requiring users to understand use of the
services at only a rudimentary level. Unintentional or
malicious data leakage can take place via the same actions
individuals use on any given day in order to do their job:
uploading data to or downloading data from Cloud services.

When the data is in the Cloud, who actually owns it? Is it
the user, the company subscribing to the Cloud, or the
organization that is providing the Cloud services? Could a
Cloud provider actually deny a client access to their own

data? These are critical questions to address, related to the following top three security concerns for data in the Cloud:

1. Lack of control over the data location
2. Increased vulnerability on account of shared infrastructures
3. Privileged user abuse at the Cloud services provider.

Everything within the virtual stack – the hypervisors*, storage, and data – may be vulnerable. Traditional system administrators find trying to understand how to deploy and manage virtual technologies challenging. Organizations have granted virtual system administrators the keys to their kingdoms. This new, super-privileged group has unfettered access to everything within their virtual environment.

What are the primary Cloud-related insider threat concerns? Research by Claycomb and Nicoll identified three primary types of Cloud-related insider threats:[78]

1. Rouge Cloud administrator. The rogue administrator is likely the most common vector for a Cloud-based insider threat. Motivations include financial gain, grudges against the provider or the organization, or retribution for an actual or perceived harm. Below is a summary of a rogue Cloud administrator case study from the CMU SEI database of insider threats:

   The case involves a system administrator (SA) in a data mining company contracted to process customer

---

* A hypervisor is a type of software that allows an information system to manage more than one operating system (OS). It uses a process called virtualization to trick the OS into thinking that it has exclusive use of a particular set of hardware and applications. It sits between the physical hardware and the OS and manages the flow of information between the software, virtualized hardware, and physical hardware. For more information, see *www.webopedia.com/quick_ref/hypervisor.asp*.

information. The SA had access to servers and data owned by the customer and found an unprotected file with encrypted password information on one of the servers. The SA used brute force to attack over 300 passwords and accessed data belonging to dozens of customers, allowing him to download millions of personal records.[79]

Cloud SAs as insider threat not only have the ability to exfiltrate data, they also have the ability to impact data availability by restricting access to the Cloud.

2. Employee in the victim organization. This is the most overlooked form of insider threat. It involves an insider within the organization who intentionally exploits vulnerabilities in the Cloud service or unintentionally allows access. Motivations for the intentional insider are similar to those of the rogue administrator. The unintentional insider threat is often successful because they are enabled by ineffective security policies and procedures. The CMU SEI Insider Threat Database describes the following case study involving an unintentional insider threat and a phishing attack:

A malicious outsider tricked an employee in the target organization into opening an attachment infected with malware. The malware infected the target organization's information systems, allowing the attacker to gain access to the email services provided by the Cloud and exfiltrate sensitive data. The target organization noticed the attack in progress, but was unable to act quickly enough to prevent data loss.[80]

3. Insider who uses Cloud resources to carry out attacks against the company or other external organizations. This insider threat has some similarities to the above insider, but in this case the insider uses the Cloud itself as the instrument to carry out attacks on internal systems or external organizations. One of the cases in the CMU

SEI Insider Threat Database involved an insider, who planned to leave his company and leveraged access to the Cloud to launch a distributed denial-of-service (DDOS) attack against his organization. In other cases, insiders used external Cloud storage to exfiltrate and store company-owned sensitive data. One of the primary examples of this type of attack is Snowden, who moved his exfiltrated files to a secure, private Cloud location.

Big Data Security Concerns

Data security fears may be the most challenging barrier to Cloud adoption. Big Data is "the common term used to describe the deluge of data in today's networked, digitized, sensor-laden, and information-driven world."[81] Big Data is increasingly being stored in Cloud infrastructures.

Big Data combined with the Cloud magnifies insider threat, since insiders may be able to access a large amount of data with a small amount of effort. Since data is the most precious organizational asset, it is clear that an organization will want to know that its data is safe. When data is stored internally, organizations may have a (false) level of confidence that their data is secure. In fact, there is no guarantee that internal data is better protected that data in the Cloud, but there are some critical questions that are specific to the use of the Cloud for Big Data:

- Who has access to the data at the Cloud provider location? What are the Cloud provider access control policies?

- Is the data encrypted on the Cloud systems? Who holds the encryption key?

- What is the Cloud provider's business continuity plan? Is the data replicated across multiple data centers located in various geographical locations?
- What is the data backup process? Where is it stored?
- Is there a data recovery process?
- What are the incident detection, reporting, and handling processes? Who is responsible for investigating a security breach?

These questions highlight the fact that security and privacy controls for Big Data necessitate a very different approach to that used for traditional networked systems. Traditional security approaches that relied heavily on boundary protection defenses at local, firewalled and semi-isolated networks will no longer be sufficient to provide security to Big Data environments.

The three V's of Big Data – velocity, variety and volume – elevate Big Data security concerns, and require new approaches. **Velocity** describes the tempo at which data is transferred, handled, and stored – in Big Data, information arrives in large batches or is continuously streamed across distributed locations. The speed of the data transfers, combined with a weakened security boundary, can result in unwanted data leaks. The consequence is an enhanced requirement for the enforcement of strong authentication mechanisms across geographically distributed nodes.

Variety refers to the organization of the data and the fact that Big Data is drawn from a number of diverse sources, creating an environment that is largely organically grown and has not been designed with security in mind. While each source may have data protections in place or use anonymized data sets, Big Data may be able to correlate these datasets with other public databases leading to 'de-anonymization'.[82]

Volume is used to describe the amount of data. In terms of Big Data, this can easily range from gigabytes to terabytes and more. By virtue of the sheer volume of Big Data, storage is multi-layered and often distributed, resulting in the need for equally multi-layered and distributed security protections.

The Bottom Line with Cloud and Big Data: Increased Loss of Control

With Cloud computing, an organization has to come to terms with the fact that they no longer have direct control of the IT infrastructure and information. There are two primary loss of control types: technical and organizational. Technical loss of control refers to access control, software updates and version control, and control over the execution of backup and restoration activities. Organizational loss of control is related mainly to the human factors. These range from fear of loss of importance to the organization, job loss, and the pure fear of change. It is this loss of organizational control that provides the primary access path for both the intentional and unintentional insider threat.

FedRAMP - US Efforts to Secure the Cloud against Insider Threat

Several years ago, the US General Services Administration (GSA) initiated the Federal Risk and Authorization Management Program (FedRAMP) to specifically address the security challenges of the Cloud. FedRAMP protections are based on NIST Special Publication 800-53, *Security and*

Privacy Controls for Federal Information Systems and Organizations. FedRAMP required Cloud service providers desiring to do business with the Federal Government to meet security controls specifically selected to protect Cloud environments.

Analysis of recent insider threat activities has prompted the US Government to introduce a number of changes to the existing process, to include additional penetration testing requirements, or stringent controls over mobile devices, malicious user testing, auditing of privileged functions, and enhanced insider threat security training requirements for Cloud providers.

The renewed efforts also include an increased emphasis on compliance by 'interconnected systems', or those that are connected to but not within the Cloud provider boundary. These interconnected systems must now comply with all of the same regulations and safeguards as those within the provider boundary. While these requirements are not perfect by any means, FedRAMP represents an effort on a large scale to recognize and address the security challenges associated with large Cloud service providers.

Recommendations for Additional Reading
NIST Big Data Interoperability Framework: Volume 4, Security and Privacy. NIST Special Publication 1500-4, September 2015.
McDonald, Kevin T. February 2010. *Above the Clouds – Managing Risk in the World of Cloud Computing*. IT Governance Publishing, Cambridgeshire, UK
U.S. General Services Administration FedRAMP Program at *www.fedramp.gov/*.

CHAPTER 5: REGIONAL PERSPECTIVES ON INSIDER THREAT

There are so many people in the world with so many different perspectives. – *Dave Sitek[83]

The perspective about how to approach data protection varies across the globe. This is a result of a combination of regulatory and legal controls, as well as cultural differences.

Globalization has added a new dynamic to the insider threat. In a global operational environment, organizations must expand inside access and knowledge of their internal operations to a new population that may have a different perspective on insider behavior, and who are much less verifiable. Employees in other countries may be faced with a conflict between cultural and national allegiances and the corporate values and priorities.

The obstacles to global organizations are numerous. The legal infrastructure in many countries may not offer any deterrent to insider betrayal. Cultural norms and legal protections for privacy and intellectual ownership vary significantly between nations. "Of all the data losses reported by the UK Government… only 5% is believed to be due to technology whilst 95% is due to cultural factors."[84]

A global supply chain has also increased the potential for an expanded insider threat, whether physical or digital. For example, many countries have their products assembled in

---

* Dave Sitek is an American musician and guitarist.

another country, which carries with it the potential for the insertion of an item intended to do harm. Software code is often written in foreign countries, opening up the aperture for malicious code to be inserted into an application and then later exploited.

Considering all of the potential threat avenues, it is critical to understand the regional perspectives and cultural differences that influence the understanding of insider threat and the implementation of mitigating measures. The 2015 Vormetric report on insider threat highlights some of these critical differences in perspective and how these influence national approaches.[85] The CMU SEI has conducted additional analysis on regional and national approaches to insider threat mitigation.[86] Most importantly, each region must select its insider threat mitigation strategies based on its unique perceptions, policies, and threats.

By most accounts, there are currently 196 countries in the world. In each of these, regional perspectives and cultural attitudes about insider threat and security differ significantly. Western nations, such as the US, the UK, and Germany, may find it difficult to understand that "acceptable norms for doing business also differ according to region. Practices that are considered illegal in the Western world ... may be a common and accepted practice in some regions."[87]

It is not possible to provide examples from every one of the 190-plus nations, so a set of representative nations has been chosen to highlight how perspectives of insider threat may differ across the globe. The nations below have been selected as examples based on several factors: (1) the maturity level of their communications infrastructure;

(2) the existence of a certain degree of regulation and law enforcement that acknowledges insider threat; (3) the extent to which national cultural perspectives either contribute to or restrict communications; and (4) the likelihood of 'acceptable' corruption being present.

Regional Perspectives – Different Views on Insider Threat

United States

According to the Vormetric 2015 report[88] on insider threat, the United States reports a significantly higher level of anxiety than in other nations. This is likely on account of the large number of public breaches within the past two years, ranging from the Target department store hack to the data exfiltrations perpetrated by Snowden and Manning. Much of the interest in insider threat in the US is driven by the highly public and damaging national security incidents, together with the well-publicized private sector breaches. In fact, "44% of North American organizations suffered from a serious security breach ... during the last 12 months."[89] While not all of these were perpetrated by direct insiders, all of them involved either an actual insider, a third-party vendor, or the external exploitation of an insider. All of these events have left public and private organizations feeling vulnerable to insider attacks. This high level of concern is most apparent when the US is compared with European nations, such as Germany and the UK, where worries appear to be centered on criminal acts such as fraud and identity theft.

Germany

Germany has an advanced cybersecurity capability and a strong history of security and privacy regulations. Germany takes a proactive approach to protection from insider threats and, as a result, Germans tend to value their vulnerability to malicious insider activity lower than any other country. According to the Vormetric report, "no single German organization said that it was extremely vulnerable to insider attacks."[90]

Yet despite this general feeling of invincibility, Germany has been the site of significant data breaches. In fact, Germany ranks among the "top five countries in terms of the number of malicious cyber activities."[91] Another cultural factor impacting German perception of insider threat is a historic distrust of informants, which results in a reluctance to report potential insider threat activity.

Japan

Japanese culture is largely heterogeneous and peer pressure is quite high, meaning that Japanese organizations tend to default to trust. As a result, Japan is a remarkable exception to the widely accepted norm that privileged users are the group that poses the greatest threat to an enterprise. In fact, the Vormetric report indicated that 56% of the organizations polled felt that ordinary users were the greatest threat, with contractors and service providers coming in a close second at 52%.[92] The underlying reason for this difference likely lies in Japanese culture itself, which fosters a belief that employees are loyal and trustworthy by nature and that insider threat activities are unthinkable.

United Kingdom

The UK demonstrates a far greater concern about insider threat than other European countries. While many nations indicated that data breaches were of greatest concern, the Vormetric report found that the UK was the only country where Cloud computing environments were seen as the greatest risk.[93] This is largely a result of the UK's strong acceptance of Cloud computing as a viable alternative to local data storage. The UK also has a high level of concern about insider threats and fraud and identity theft. The Vormetric survey indicated that more than 40% of UK businesses consider that it is privileged users (system administrators, database administrators, network administrators, etc.) that constitute the biggest risk to their organizations.[94]

But data breaches and the Cloud computing environment are not the only insider threat concern in the UK. Others are based less on the digital environment, and more on terrorist-based insider events. Recently, the UK has raised its terrorist-related insider threat levels in response to a rise in British Muslims estimated to have joined groups like ISIS.[95]

India

India has a heterogeneous culture comprised of over 18 major and 48 minor groups (as identified by language). Nonetheless, there are some homogenous cultural characteristics. Primary among these are India's rather collectivist perspectives, where interpersonal relationships and trust are rated highly.

Like Japan, the Flynn report indicates the respect and approval of one's family members, supervisors and peers are sought after. Despite this cultural tendency, corruption and fraud "... appear to be embedded in political, economic, and sociocultural facets of Indian Society."[96] Corruption, usually in the form of bribery, is also common. Employees and partners are most likely to become insider threats when they perceive that organizations are not acting in accordance with the collectivist norm.

Russia

Many nations, including the US, sometimes see Russia as a source of insider threat – however, Russia itself is one of the most recent victims of a terrorist-related insider threat. On 31 October 2015, Metrojet Flight 9268, carrying more than 200 passengers and crew, disintegrated over the Sinai desert in Egypt. Russian investigation indicates that the crash came about as a result of an insider that placed a bomb somewhere in the tail section of the aircraft. Initial theories seem to point to someone with privileged access "to airport food service and flight line activities, rather than a passenger who was required to go through airport screening."[97]

Despite being one of the newest victims of insider threat, the Vormetric research reveals Russian internal and external policies tend to rely heavily on a competitive stance versus the West. At its core, Russian culture has been traditionally authoritarian. A recurring historical trend is the tendency to engage in any actions that can be viewed as a means to achieve certain national goals. This culture places a very high value on the homeland and family. Further, it is a watchful culture, so an insider displaying some of the characteristics and patterns noted in *Chapter 2* is more likely to be quickly noticed and neutralized. Russia is often viewed from the outside as a closed, personal culture and many of the values, such as *pravda, dusha* and *krug** are an enigma to much of the Western world.

Recommendations for Additional Reading
Goodman, Marc. *Future Crimes: Everything is Connected, Everyone is Vulnerable, and What We Can Do About It.* February 2015. Doubleday Publishing.

---

* *Pravda,* which can be translated as truth, is a concept of what it just or fair and serves as a moral guideline; *dusha* refers to the Russian concept of soul, or the core of being; and *krug* is the concept of Russian friendship as a close circle that is not easily formed, but once formed, not easily broken.

CHAPTER 6: BEST PRACTICES, CONTROLS AND QUICK WINS

*Innovation and best practices can be sown throughout an organization – but only when they fall on fertile ground. – *Marcus Buckingham[98]*

It may be possible to stop the employee who could become an insider threat, but it is not a simple problem. It requires a layered approach, incorporating policies, procedures and technical controls. Organizations must realize that this is not an IT issue, but rather a reflection of overall business processes, organizational culture, and the underlying technologies. There are also some quick, but potentially high impact, fixes that can be applied as organizations ramp up to a more comprehensive insider threat program.

Preventing all insider threats may not be economically feasible, or even possible. Effective and practical approaches to mitigating insider threat must be based on each organization's unique risk management strategy. So here is the critical question: If an organization as secure as the US National Security Agency (NSA) is unable to protect its top secret data from a 28-year-old contract employee named Snowden with less than three months on the job, how can any other organization hope to defend itself from the malicious insider?

If there is one thing that the Snowden exposure demonstrates, it is that absolute security is nearly

---

* Marcus Buckingham is a best-selling British-American author and motivational speaker.

impossible to attain and can be compromised by a trusted insider. After-the-fact damage assessments, however, also show that indicators that can be recognized exist, and that there are technologies and processes organizations can use to make themselves more secure and more resistant to insider threats.

Technology is Not a Silver Bullet

Faced with this challenge, many organizations see protections via new technologies as a potential silver bullet.* But can technology alone solve all the problems? The answer is clear. Although many technologies exist to enforce access rights, privileges, and policies, the technology is only as good as the people using it and the processes that are implemented and followed. If the individuals who control these technologies decide to circumvent the system's ability to enforce policies, or to make an exception, or ignore violations, or not to enforce sufficient supervisory mechanisms, then the technology alone will inevitably fall short.

Unfortunately, even today organizations tend to focus on low level technologies, such as automated vulnerability scans, as a primary means to mitigate threats. Although technology solutions may solve part of the problem, they do not represent a complete approach to addressing insider threat concerns. Conventional practices, such as employee background checks or even security clearances, have also not proven successful when used in isolation.

---

* The term 'silver bullet' is often used to refer to anything that offers a simple and seemingly magical solution to a difficult and complex problem. The use of the term allegedly derives from the widespread belief that silver bullets were able to kill werewolves or other supernatural beings.

It's likewise crucial to consider the possible insider risk posed not only by direct employees, but also by other organizations and individuals with which an organization collaborates, such as partners, contractors, consultants, or any form of association that provides access to organizational assets. This last group can include those responsible for supplying an organization's physical facility, as well as its networks, information systems, and information.

There is clearly no single, quick solution that will completely eliminate the risk of an insider threat. However, following a large number of high profile incidents, such as Manning, Snowden and the terrorist events in San Bernardino, focused research after the fact has resulted in a number of best practices that can assist in mitigating the possibility of insider threats. CMU SEI, for example, recommends a number of best practices that can prevent – or at least facilitate – early detection of many of the types of insider threat. These best practices are based on their research into more than 700 inside threat cases over several decades. The US Department of Defense (DoD) has also developed a number of initiatives as a result of their post-mortems of the Snowden and Manning cases. Industry-sponsored research by organizations including the Gartner Group and Ponemon, has also contributed a number of recommendations. The best practices below represent a synthesis of CMU SEI research, US Government and DoD insider threat analysis, and several other research products from industry and industry-sponsored researchers.

It will soon become clear that implementation of these practices does not fall exclusively to the IT department. Rather, the success of these measures relies on the cooperative engagement of multiple elements across an organization.

- Human Resources (HR)

- Physical/Facility Security

- Information Technology (IT)/Cybersecurity (CS)

- Management/Information Owners (IO)

- Legal

- Security/Software (S/SW) Engineering

Adapting the format applied in the CMU SEI *Common Sense Guide to Mitigating Insider Threats*, each recommended practice – described below in more detail – is headed by a graphic table indicating which of the departments listed above have starring roles in executing that practice. One important note – these organizational elements may be highlighted, but that does not mean that other agency elements should be neglected. Additional contributors can include section supervisors and individuals from sections such as business continuity, auditing, finance, public relations, quality assurance, and training. The list is only limited by the desire of the organization to create a fully integrated insider threat program, and the willingness of the staff elements to participate in the effort.

Research into the insider threat by the Intelligence and National Security Alliance revealed that, at bottom, there are three primary and fairly simple practices implemented by organizations that demonstrate a good degree of success in establishing effective insider threat programs:

1. An effective insider threat program extends beyond perimeter protection tools for monitoring network traffic or online activity. It incorporates non-technical processes and procedures, as well as technical tools, to develop and maintain a holistic view of the insider threat risk by identifying and taking action on anomalous, suspicious, or otherwise concerning non-technical behavior patterns.

2. Organizations with mature and successful insider threat programs have visible buy-in from senior leadership.

3. The insider threat program rests on solid partnerships and engagement between Human Resources, Cybersecurity/IT staff, Legal Counsel, Physical and Facilities Security, and Executive Leadership.[99]

It's important to note that the list of best practices presented in the following sections, while comprehensive, will not necessarily be appropriate for each organization. Consideration must be given to the organization's needs and culture. Also, no organization has the resources or funds to ensure 100% protection against all threats to its assets. Sometimes, it is essential to focus initially on a quick win rather than longer-term solutions. Each best practice below will include a section on quick wins – or low hanging fruit – that could bring a good return in detecting, deterring, and recovering from insider threats without overly extensive resources or a long lead time.

The measures are logically organized based on a layered approach that moves from high level strategic and programmatic actions to operational implementations, as follows: policy and strategic initiatives; personnel security and management; training and awareness; deterrence; detection and protection; and reaction, response and recovery.

Any best practice should be supported by one or more existing standards. Each section will also include a mapping to: The National Institute of Standards (NIST) Special Publication (SP) 800-53, *Security Controls for Federal Information Systems and Organizations*; ISO/IEC 27001:2013, Information technology – Security techniques – Information Security Management Systems-Requirements; and ISO/IEC 27002:2013, Information technology – Security techniques – Code of practice for information security controls. This by no means indicates that these are the *only* standards and processes that an organization can use to obtain implementation guidance; it is merely a nod to a selection of standards that are both comprehensive and internationally accepted. One final note – certain security controls are highlighted from each of the standards; however, each organization may wish to broaden its look at the standards and consider other security controls as possible supporting measures to mitigate the insider threat problem.

Policy and Strategic Initiatives

1. Institute a Formal Insider Threat (InT) Program

According to research by the INSA Cyber Insider Threat Task Force, "just over half of the organizations interviewed have a formal Insider Threat mitigation program. These programs are quite diverse, illustrating the need for a more widely accepted definition of what a formal Insider Threat mitigation program is."[100]

A formal insider threat program cannot be solely technology-focused. The many forms of available technology are usually intended to identify and restrict outsider access, using products such as firewalls and intrusion detection systems (IDS). Why is this the case? Attacks from outside are generally easier to detect and defend against. The insider threat problem is much harder to address. A study by the Ponemon Institute revealed that at least 60% of executives and security professionals are unable to assess or quantify the insider Threat, even though they may realize that the insider can pose a dire risk to the organization.[101]

So, is a formal insider threat program necessary? The answer is a resounding yes! "A formalized program codifies the mission, intent, scope, implementation, and oversight of the organization's insider threat efforts. The formal program provides a measurable response to insider attacks and can show the organization's progress in mitigating insider attacks. Additionally, a formal program creates the opportunity for resources [to be] dedicated to Insider Threat mitigation, an essential step in building a successful Insider Threat program."[102]

Insider threats are human beings – and an effective program must integrate technical and non-technical processes with elements of all of the best practices listed below:

- Senior leadership support for the insider threat program must be active and visible.

- Insider threat mitigation efforts must be incorporated into processes and synchronized across all departments in the organization.

- The InT program must include an integrated capability to monitor and audit for insider threat activity, which involves gathering, integrating, reviewing, assessing, and responding to information from across the organization.

- Appropriate insider threat training, education and awareness should be made available to all employees, consultants, contractors and partners with access to the corporate resources.

- The collection, use, maintenance and dissemination of insider threat information must comply with all of the applicable local, state, and national laws, including those regarding privacy and whistleblower and civil liberty protections.

There are a number of possible key components in an effective insider threat program. In the CMU SEI Insider Threat Blog posted on 11 March 2015, Matt Collins provided an illustrative graphic that highlights the components that the CMU SEI has defined as the most

critical to establishing and maintaining a fully functional
and comprehensive insider threat program (*Figure 12*).[103]

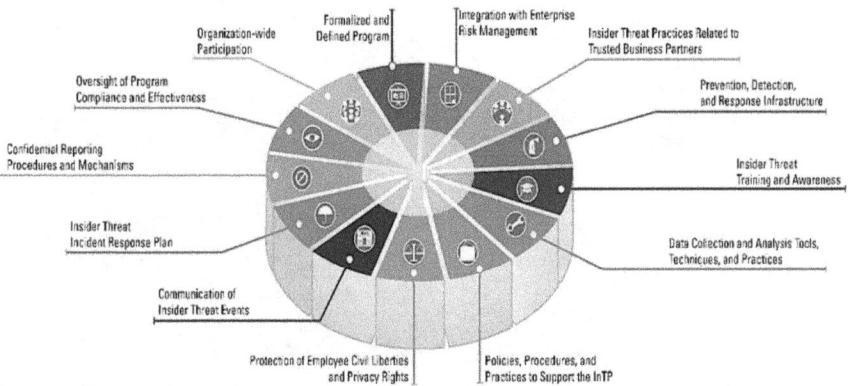

Source: CMU SEI CERT Insider Threat Blog, https://insights.sei.cmu.edu/insider-
threat/2015/03/intp-series-key-elements-of-an-insider-threat-program-part-2-of-18.html

Figure 12: Key components of an insider threat program

Now that the key components of an InT program have been
visually illustrated, how does an organization go about
building one? *Figure 13* provides a step-by-step logical
approach.

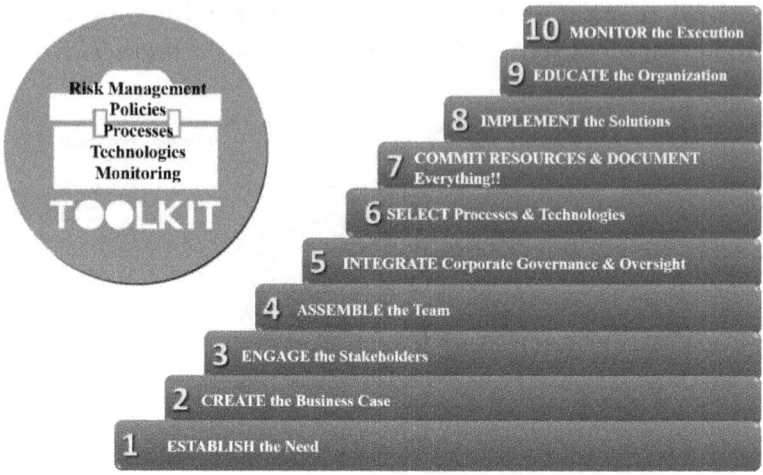

Figure 13: 10 Steps to an insider threat program

While the key components illustrated in *Figure 12* and the 10 steps in *Figure 13* may be commonly accepted as a standard, their actual implementation must be customized for each organization's mission, operations, and culture.

An effective insider threat program must involve recurring activity – it is not a one-time action. Establishing the program is certainly important, but it is equally important to regularly bring together the associated organizational elements to evaluate the success of the tools and technologies, processes and procedures. The purpose is to keep and continue to maintain activities that are producing positive results, while reducing or eliminating those that are showing less return on organizational security investment.

One final note: when designing, implementing, and monitoring the insider threat program, remember the ancient Latin expression *'Quis Custodiet Ipsos Custodos?'* – Who watches the watchers? A successful program must include carefully thought-out oversight, approved by legal counsel, which provides sufficient assurance at all levels in the organization that the program will maintain a strict adherence to guidelines approved by regulators and legislators.

The Quick Wins

- Obtain buy-in from the critical organizational elements: senior leadership, legal counsel, human resources, facility and physical security, privacy officer, and cyber/IT security.
- Identify and prioritize the organizational assets that need protection, with the understanding that not everything can be defended with equal effect.
- Follow the 10-step process for creating and managing a formal InT program.
- Ensure that legal counsel reviews and approves the appropriate legal and regulatory frameworks for the program.
- Create an oversight program, assign responsibilities, disseminate information about reporting processes and ensure the program is implemented equitably and in compliance with local, state, and federal laws and regulations.

Standards Mapping

STANDARD	CONTROL	SUBJECT
NIST 800-53, Rev 4, Security Controls for Federal Information Systems and Organizations	PL-1	Security Planning Policy and Procedures
	PL-7	Security Concept pf Operations
	PM-12	Insider Threat Program

STANDARD	CONTROL	SUBJECT
ISO/IEC 27001:2013, Information technology – Security techniques – Information Security Management Systems – Requirements	A.6.1.1	Management commitment to information security
	A.15.1	Compliance with legal requirements
	A.15.1.5	Prevention of misuse of information processing facilities
ISO/IEC 27002:2013, Information technology – Security techniques – Code of practice for information security management	6.1.2	Information security coordination
	15.1.5	Prevention of misuse of information processing facilities

Recommendations for Additional Reading
Capelli, Dawn; Moore, Andrew; and Trzeciak, Randall. *The CERT Guide to Insider Threats: How to Prevent, Detect, and Respond to Information Technology Crimes (Theft, Sabotage, Fraud).* SEI Series in Software Engineering. January 2012. Addison Wesley Publishing Company.
Zinatullin, Leron. *The Psychology of Information Security – Resolving conflicts between security compliance and human behaviour.* January 2016. IT Governance Publishing.

2. Exercise Enterprise-Wide Risk Management – Know What Needs Protection and Manage the Risk

Let's keep this simple: risk is the likelihood of loss or damage. Risk management is the life-cycle approach to keeping risk at an acceptable level. No organization has sufficient resources to implement 100% protective measures and completed eradicate any risk, and no organization has exactly the same appetite or tolerance* for risk. As such, it is critical to direct efforts towards protecting those assets that are critical to the organization and not to spend unnecessary resources to defend less important data and resources.

Before initiating any actions, the organization must develop its own unique definition of 'adequate security'. There are a number of questions an organization can ask to help it understand the risk and define what level of security is considered sufficient:

- What are the assets and the value we must protect? Value can be obtained from tangible assets – such as a product, information, or service – or intangibles, such as reputation.

---

* Risk appetite or risk tolerance refers to the broad level of risk an organization and its leadership is willing or able to accept, and what level of security is considered adequate to address that risk. The risk tolerance/appetite determination is essentially a leadership responsibility.

- Why must we protect this value and these assets? What is the impact if they are not protected?

- What potential consequences must be mitigated? At what cost? Is there a cost-benefit equation? How much damage can be tolerated before action is essential?

- What is the residual risk (the risk remaining after mitigation measures are implement) and how can this residual risk be effectively managed?

- How can the answers to these questions be integrated into an effective, sustainable, and enforceable security program?

By executing an enterprise-wide risk assessment, organizations are better able to identify critical assets and potential threat agents, and to assess the likelihood of a threat agent successfully exploiting a vulnerability plus the associated impact. The results of the risk assessment can be used to develop or refine an overall risk management strategy for the organization's assets.

Executing the Risk Assessment and Analysis

Conducting a risk assessment and the associated analysis is not a trivial effort. Unfortunately, risk is a much-misunderstood concept and there are as many ways to conduct a risk assessment and analysis as there are definitions for risk itself. That said, all of the risk assessment methodologies essentially break down into two approaches: quantitative and qualitative.

Quantitative risk assessment focuses on two fundamentals: the probability of an event and the likely impact should it occur. It makes use of one of two concepts, 'Annual Loss

Expectancy' (ALE) or 'Estimated Annual Cost' (EAC), each of which is calculated for each individual event. The primary drawback to the quantitative approach is the unreliability, lack of consistency and inaccuracy of the data. Such things as probability can rarely be precisely measured.

The qualitative approach to evaluating risk is more widely used. Qualitative assessments rely on a number of interrelated elements – including 'assets', 'vulnerability', 'threat or threat agent', 'likelihood', 'impact', 'risk', and 'residual risk' – that must be understood, including the relationship between them.

> Risk assessment is the overall process of risk identification, risk analysis, and risk evaluation.
>
> ISO/IEC 31010:2009

The following definitions are adapted from NIST Special Publication 800-30* and ISO/IEC 31000:2009*:

- Asset: a person, capability, or resource whose value can be measured.

- Threat or threat agent: a natural, environmental, or human potential to accidentally spark or intentionally exploit a vulnerability.

---

* NIST Special Publication (SP) 800-30, Revision 1, *Risk Management Guide for Information Technology Systems*, is a standard developed by the US National Institute of Standards and Technology and is a guide to conducting risk assessments and analysis, largely focused on Federal information systems.
* ISO/IEC 31000:2009, Risk Management – Principles and guidelines is a standard issued by the International Organization for Standardization (ISO), which provides generic guidance on techniques for risk management.

- Vulnerability: a flaw or weakness in procedures, design, implementation, or internal controls that could be exploited by a threat/threat agent.
- Likelihood: the probability that an event or situation will occur.
- Impact: the effect or consequence the organization will experience if the threat/threat agent is successful.
- Risk: a function of the likelihood of a given threat/threat agent initiating or exploiting a vulnerability and the resulting impact on the organization.
- Residual risk: the risk that remains after efforts have been undertaken to mitigate the identified risks.

Although there are numerous methods for executing a risk assessment and analysis, most follow some common steps:

Step 1: Identify and document assets – develop a description of the organization/system(s) and the assets necessary to fulfil the organization's mission. This step provides the foundation for the subsequent risk assessment phases.

Step 2: Identify and document threats – compile a list of potential dangers to the organization/system(s), which can be environmental, human, natural or technical. Environmental threats include power failure, chemicals, or liquid leakage. Human threats are enabled or caused by humans and may be intentional or unintentional. Natural threats include floods, earthquakes, hurricanes and other natural disasters. NIST SP 800-30, *Risk Management Guide for Information Systems*, provides a fairly comprehensive starting list of possible threat agents to organizations and information systems. For most organizations, the human threat – or the insider – will cause the greatest concern. After the list of all possible threat agents is developed, the organization should reduce the list to only those threats that can be reasonably anticipated. For example, a hurricane may be a significant threat to the coastal communities of Florida, but is clearly less threatening to an organization based in Idaho.

> A vulnerability of an asset triggered or exploited by a threat agent equals a risk. A threat must have the capability to trigger or exploit a weakness in order to create risk.

Step 3: Determine and document vulnerabilities – identify weaknesses that could lead to a security event or an incident. This process is similar to that of identifying threat agents. The organization creates a comprehensive list of all weaknesses, associated with their operations and information systems. Vulnerabilities can be grouped into two primary categories: technical and non-technical. Technical weaknesses may be misconfigurations, flaws or defects in an information system or an organization's perimeter. Non-technical weaknesses may stem from non-existent or ineffective policies, procedures, and standards. Sources of information for technical vulnerabilities may include vulnerability scans of the system or publicly available lists and advisories from vendors or from public or commercial computer incident response teams. Non-technical vulnerability lists may come from previous risk analyses, audit reports, or security review reports.
The Internet is a great resource for discovering technical weaknesses and for sharing vulnerability lists and advisories.

Step 4: Evaluate likelihood of occurrence – likelihood can be expressed in terms of frequency of occurrence for each individual vulnerability and threat pair. The greater the likelihood, the higher the risk. Quantifying likelihood can be difficult, but there are factors that can be used to assist in defining the likelihood – likelihood can be based on a number of factors that include motivation, presence, history, capability and environment. An example might be expressed in this way: asset = information network; threat agent = unintentional insider; weakness = lack of training. The likelihood of a threat agent, such as a Chinese rival, exploiting a weakness, such as a naïve insider, might be considered very high based on capability, history, and motivation. *Figure 14* defines levels of likelihood and a tentative associated value.

Likelihood	Description	Value
Almost Never	It is difficult for a threat agent to exploit the vulnerability or it is not expected to occur within 5 years.	1
Possible, but Unlikely	It is feasible, but would require significant skills or resources or it is expected to occur within 3-5 years.	2
Possible	It is feasible for the threat to exploit the vulnerability or it may occur within 12-36 months.	3
Highly Likely	It is feasible for the threat agent to exploit the vulnerability using minimal skills or resources or may occur within 6-12 months.	4
Almost Certain	It is easy for the threat agent to exploit the vulnerability without any unique skills or resources and may occur frequently.	5

Figure 14: Levels of likelihood

Step 5: Determine severity of impact – impact on the organization if the threat agent is successful and exploits an associated vulnerability of set of vulnerabilities. The severity of impact is evaluated with *no* controls in place. This informs the gross risk rating and better enables the organization to determine the effectiveness of security controls to mitigate the risk. Using the same example above, the impact of Chinese hackers exploiting the network through social engineering of a naïve insider and gaining access to the corporate network to steal intellectual property could easily be rated as serious. *Figure 15* defines levels of impact severity and an associated value.

Impact	Description	Value
Insignificant	Little or no impact	1
Minor	Minimal effort to repair, restore, or reconfigure	2
Significant	Small, but tangible harm, maybe noticeable by a limited audience, some embarrassment, some effort to repair	3
Damaging	Damage to reputation, loss of confidence, significant effort o repair	4
Serious	Considerable outage, loss of customers, business confidence, compromise of large amount of information	5
Critical	Extended outage, permanent loss of asset, triggering of business continuity plan, complete compromise of information	5

Figure 15: Levels of severity impact

Step 6: Determine risk levels – level of risk can be determined by analyzing the values assigned to the likelihood of each threat occurrence, and the resulting impact if a weakness is exploited. The raw or inherent risk is derived by multiplying the likelihood by the impact. Again following the example above, with a likelihood of very high (5) and an impact of serious (5), the raw risk would be 25. *Figure 16* presents a sample 5x5 matrix for assigning a risk rating by mapping likelihood and impact.

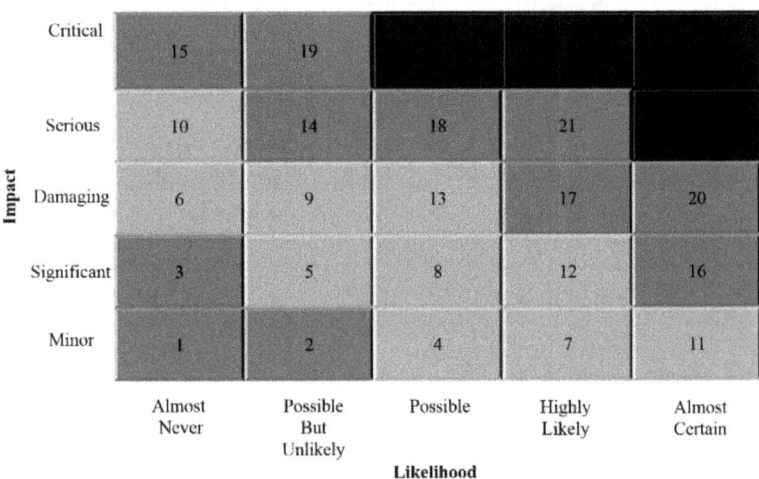

Figure 16: Raw risk matrix

Step 7: Identify controls in place – controls can be operational, such as change management, or technical, such as access control, system patching, or boundary protection devices. A control can reduce the risk by reducing the likelihood and/or the impact of an event. Controls should be mapped to one or more risks. Note that, if controls have been identified but cannot be mapped to a specific risk, it is important to evaluate whether or not they are providing value and if these controls really need to be implemented. The second component of this step is to determine if the controls are operating effectively. The figure below[2*] illustrates the components of risk assessment and analysis and the type of security controls most effective in addressing that risk.

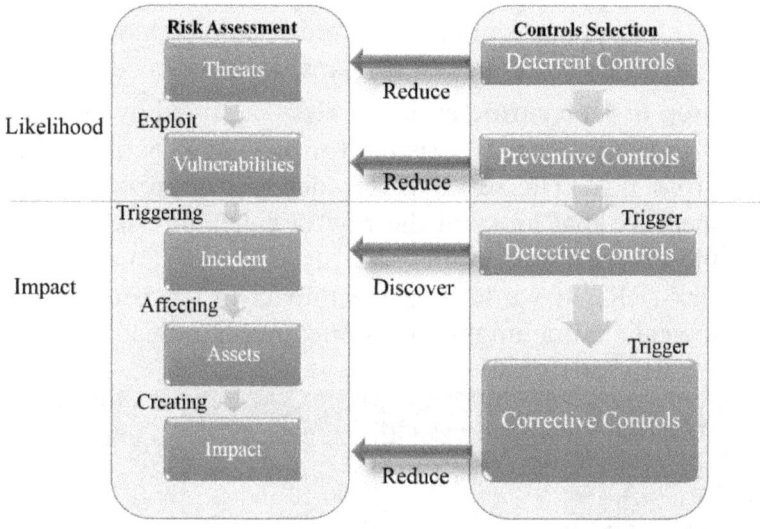

Figure 17: Assessment process and controls selection

The following represents a brief description and examples of each type of control highlighted in *Figure 17*:

- Deterrent controls are intended to discourage a potential threat agent. Examples include security awareness training, security cameras, or a security policy.
- Preventive controls are designed to mitigate the likelihood of an incident. Examples include restricting privileged user access, configuring firewall rues, or limiting access to a restricted area.

---

* Adapted from Sherwood, Clark and Lynas, *Enterprise Security Architecture: A Business-Driven Approach*, 2005.

- Detective controls are used to identify when an event has occurred. An intrusion detection system is typical of a detective control.
- Corrective controls are designed to execute repairs after an incident has occurred. These include business continuity of operations plans and system backups.

Step 8: Determine residual risk – derived by assessing the effectiveness of existing (or planned) controls on the gross risk. The residual risk determination is a simple measure that looks at the raw or inherent risk (IR) less the effectiveness of the security controls (C) = residual risk (RR). If we look at the impact in terms of dollars, the calculation might look something like this:

	Likelihood	Impact	Total
	Times	$	$
Inherent Risk	10	5000	50,000
LESS:			
Control Effectiveness	80%		
Residual Risk	2	3,000	6,000

Figure 18: Residual risk calculation example

Clearly, this is a highly simplified calculation. It becomes increasingly complex when – as is often the case – there are multiple controls addressing a single risk. There are two approaches to this. One approach would be to look at the combined effectiveness as the higher of the two controls;

the other approach would be to consider the combined control effectiveness as the total of both controls.

	Approach 1	Approach 2
Control 1	60%	60%
Control 2	30%	40%
% Reduction/ Total	60%	90%

Figure 19: Combined control effectiveness

From Risk Assessment and Analysis to Risk Management

Risk management is the core of the strategic management of any organization and is the process by which organizations methodically identify and address the most critical risks associated with their activities. It can be defined as a set of coordinated activities designed to direct an organization with regards to risk. The ability to manage risks is dependent upon the risk assessment and risk analysis process.

According to the DoD Insider Threat Report, the first element of risk management is criticality of the asset; the second, vulnerability; the third, threat. Risk happens when these three elements come together. Risk management addresses how these three elements converge in several forms:

- Assets with vulnerabilities, but unknown or limited exposure to threats.

- Assets with known vulnerabilities and known threat exposure.

- Assets with known threat, known vulnerability, but not focused on a critical asset.

- Critical assets with no known vulnerabilities, but with known threat exposure.[104]

Effective risk management must focus on those areas where there is a clear cost vs. benefit result. The greatest return on security investment (ROSI) will generally occur at the intersection where criticality, weaknesses, and vulnerabilities overlap. The risk management model in *Figure 20* illustrates where the overlap occurs.

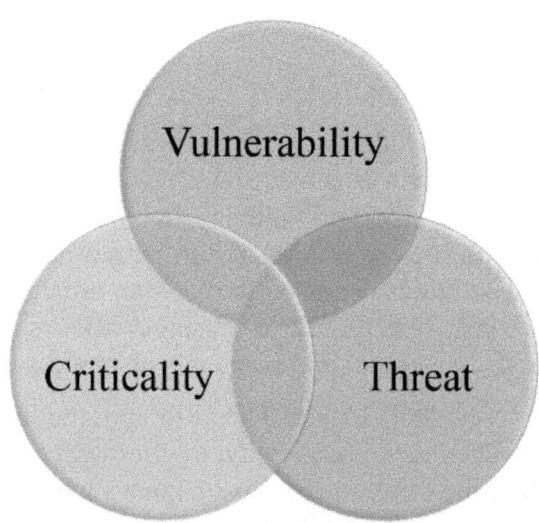

Figure 20: Risk management model

The focus of risk management activity should occur at the intersection between the areas, and the objective should be to reduce the overlap area between vulnerability, criticality, and threat.

A significant contributor to a successful risk management process is the use of SMART* criteria: specific, measurable, achievable, relevant and time-bound.

- **Specific** – the goal is clear and unambiguous.
- **Measurable** – the criteria enable measuring progress towards achievement of the goal.
- **Achievable** – the goal is realistic and attainable.
- **Relevant** – the goal must matter to the organization and to the employees.
- **Time-bound** – goals must be given a deadline and there must be commitment to that target date.

Risk management is not a one-time activity. For success, risk management must be a continuous process that is adjusted over time to address the risks associated with the organization and its operation. *Figure 21*, below, is adapted from the risk management process defined in ISO/IEC 31000 and depicts the lifecycle of risk management.

---

* The first known use of SMART as an acronym was in the 1981 issue of *Management Review* by George Doran. Over time, the letters of the acronym have meant various things depending on the author. The meanings in this text represent the most common usage.

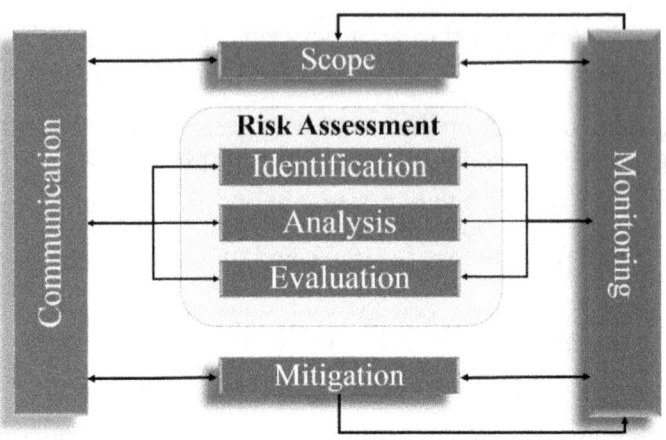

Figure 21: The risk management process (adapted from ISO/IEC 31000)

Risk management provides the policies, procedures, and organizational activities that serve to embed risk mitigation processes throughout the organization over time. The success of risk management is dependent upon **effective communications** with the stakeholders in the organization. Understanding the interests and the risk tolerance of the stakeholders is critical, and continuous communications provide the foundation. Risk tolerance varies from organization to organization and is often fraught with internal politics. It guides resource allocation and allows the organization to determine which technologies, processes, and people need to be aligned to create a structure capable of responding to and monitoring risk. At its core, risk tolerance is strategic and is an integral part of organizational governance. It is informed by the risk assessment and the risk management processes. The risk tolerance statement must come from the leaders within the organization and must be directly related to its mission (*Figure 22*).

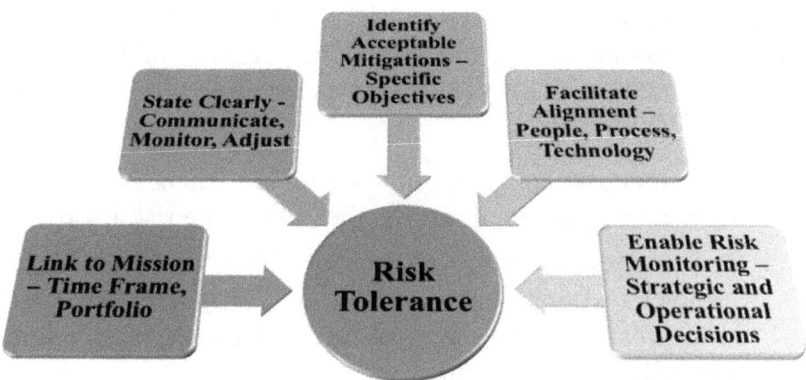

Figure 22: The risk tolerance characteristics

The **risk assessment** provides an understanding of both the raw and the residual risk. The assessment provides for an understanding of the risks, their causes and their likelihood. This critical understanding allows the organization to make the necessary decisions about:

- which risks need to be addressed;
- prioritizing risk treatment options; and
- which risk mitigations allow the overall risk to be brought to a tolerable level.

The **scope** of the risk management process sets the risk objectives, risk criteria, and determines how the risk assessment will be conducted and the extent to which the security controls are to be managed over time. Setting the scope requires an understanding of the capabilities of the organization in terms of resources and skills; the goals of the organization and the strategies that in place to achieve these goals; perceptions, values, and culture; and organizational structures.

Upon completion of the risk assessment, the risk **mitigations** involve prioritizing which risks to address and how to address them. There are essentially four types of risk mitigation strategies:

1. **Risk acceptance** is commonly adopted when the cost of the risk mitigation outweighs the cost of the risk itself.
2. **Risk avoidance** is the reverse of risk acceptance, as it involves actions intended to avoid any and all risk exposures. It is also the most resource intensive – and is generally not successful.
3. **Risk limitation** is the most prevalent strategy. The organization limits exposure by taking certain actions that are more than risk acceptance, but less than risk avoidance.
4. **Risk transference** involves handing off the risk-related actions to a third-party, such as an outsourced security service provider.

One of the most important components of risk management is **monitoring**, or reviewing the controls on a continuous basis. This is essential to verify that:

- assumptions about the individual risks remain valid;
- expected results are being achieved;
- risk mitigations are effective over time.

NIST Special Publication 800-39, *Managing Information Security Risk: Organization, Mission, and Information System View*, stresses that a three tiered approach is essential to addressing risk at the organization level, the mission/business process level, and the information system level. Risk management must be executed as seamlessly as possible across all of the tiers. *Figure 23* illustrates the three-tier approach. The organizational level establishes the risk tolerance for the organization. At the mission/business level, investment strategies and funding decisions are made. At the control implementation level, the deployment of management, operational and technical security controls is executed.

Figure 23: The 3 Tiers of risk management

It is important to note that risk management may necessitate a major organizational change in order to appropriately align the people, processes and culture with the revised goals and objectives. Culture impacts the risk management process and is reflected in the willingness to adopt leading edge processes and technologies. For example, financial institutions are more risk averse and may be inclined to look at the potential harm, rather than the benefits, of adopting new technologies. Research and development organizations, on the other hand, may be more likely to push the technological boundaries.

Together with the risk assessment and analysis, consideration of a number of these types of factors[105] (listed below) can aid in making informed risk management decisions:

- Organizational factors
  - Size (number of employees, geographic location(s) and span of operation, number of customers, size of revenue)
  - Complexity (types of products, services, processes; centralized vs. decentralized structure)
  - Intellectual property value
  - Dependence on information technology
  - Impact of disruptions or damage
  - Rate of and tolerance for organizational change
  - Stakeholder and shareholder expectations
- Market/Service sector factors
  - National and international cultural challenges
  - Customer expectation for security and privacy protections
  - Amount of service sector regulations
  - Value of reputation
  - Level of third-party relationships
  - Degree of competition

The Quick Wins

- Create an organization-specific risk assessment plan.
- Identify those individuals responsible and accountable for ensuring that the plan is executed, documented, accessible, regularly reviewed and updated.
- Involve leadership and managers in identifying assets, weaknesses, impact, and existing countermeasures as part of an enterprise-wide risk assessment.

- Ensure that weaknesses and gaps identified in the risk assessment processes are addressed and the mitigation status is reported to management.

Standards Mapping

STANDARD	CONTROL	SUBJECT
NIST 800-53, Rev 4, Security Controls for Federal Information Systems and Organizations	RA-1	Risk Assessment Policy and Procedures
	RA-3	Risk Assessment
	PM-9	Risk Management Strategy
ISO/IEC 27001:2013, Information technology – Security techniques – Information Security Management Systems – Requirements	A.7.1	Responsibility for assets
	A.7.1.1	Inventory of Assets
	A.6.2.1	Identification of risks related to external parties
	A.14.1.2	Business continuity and risk assessment
ISO/IEC 27002:2013, Information technology – Security techniques – Code of practice for information security management	8.1	Responsibility for assets
	18.2	Information security reviews
ISO/IEC 31010:2009: Risk management – risk assessment techniques	ALL	

Recommendations for Additional Reading
ISO/IEC 31010:2009 – Risk management – Risk assessment techniques.
Wheeler, Evan. *Security Risk Management: Building an Information Security Risk Management Program from the Ground Up*. May 2011. Syngress Publishing.
Landoll, Douglas J. *The Security Risk Assessment Handbook*. December 2005. CRC Press.

3. Develop, Monitor and Analyze Insider Threat Metrics

 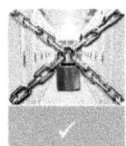    

Let's start with a clear statement – insider threat behaviors and mitigations cannot be managed if they cannot be measured. Currently, there are few metrics outside those developed by CMU SEI and US Department of Defense research to monitor and analyze insider threat behaviors and mitigations. In order to develop appropriate policies and controls and to measure their respective efficiencies and effectiveness, organizations must develop insider threat-focused metrics. The risk assessment is the first step in identifying essential measures and metrics. Other measures are generated as a means of demonstrating compliance with legislation, regulation, and policy. Additionally, a number of industry representatives, such as the Center for Internet Security (CIS) (*www.cisecurity.org/*) and the Open Web Application Security Project (OWASP)

(*www.owasp.org/index.php/Main_Page*), are creating, and implementing measures and metrics. Much of their work is publicly accessible.

The terms measures and metrics are often used interchangeably, but there is a distinction. For the purposes of this document, measures are raw data that quantify a thing that is being measured, while a metric is data processed from measures or measurements to quantify the degree to which a system or process meets a security objective.

If an organization does not develop metrics to monitor and determine the effectiveness of applied policies and controls, it may continue to make essential investment decisions based on anecdotal data, pure gut intuition, or inaccurate information – or may not make them at all. Yogi Berra* once said "You've got to be very careful if you don't know where you are going, because you might not get there."[106] The same applies to the identification and implementation of insider threat measures.

So, what exactly, is a metric? Loosely defined, a metric is a measurement that can be compared to a known scale or benchmark. Another definition is "Data used to facilitate decision-making and improve performance and accountability through collection, analysis, and reporting of relevant performance related data."[107] They are used to monitor the effectiveness of goals or objectives set for a particular focus area. They can measure the implementation

---

* Lawrence "Yogi" Berra is counted as one of the greatest US baseball players of all time during his 19-year career with the New York Yankees, and later as a coach. In addition to his career in baseball, Yogi was equally well known for his "Yogi-isms" such as "when you come to a fork in the road, take it." (*www.usatoday.com/story/sports/mlb/2015/05/12/yogi-berra-celebrates-90-birthday-yogi-isms-baseball-icon/27153095/*)

of policy, the result of services, and the impact of events on an organization's mission. Good metrics are SMART – specific, measurable, comparable, attainable, repeatable, and timely. Good metrics also provide consistency in security implementation and the ability to capture outcomes of procedures and controls with high reliability, to focus security decision making.

The purpose of measures and metrics is to transform policy into action by measuring control performance. This can only be accomplished by properly considering certain factors during the development and implementation of a security measurement and metrics analysis program:

- Data must be measurable (percentage, average, numbers);
- Data must be easily obtainable;
- Security processes measured must be repeatable;
- Performance targets must be identifiable;
- Results must provide value for tracking performance, directing resources, and introducing improvements.

In most organizations, measurements of anything related to cybersecurity are often gathered and analyzed by IT/CS personnel. However, various organizations need to be involved in their development and analysis. Management and information owners, being responsible for the overall performance of the organization, must be concerned with the ability of the organization to identify, deter, and/or respond to insider threat events.

Of course, the network and IT operations personnel are responsible for the infrastructure and its security. These personnel seek to prevent, detect and respond to network- and system-related insider threat activities. Other groups such as HR, physical and facilities security, legal counsel and engineers also have their equities in identifying and monitoring insider threat associated metrics.

Regardless of the entity or activity involved in metrics, there is a generic approach to establishing a viable metrics program. As displayed in *Figure 24*, a metrics program should be designed to evolve as security practices become fully integrated into an organization's daily operations.

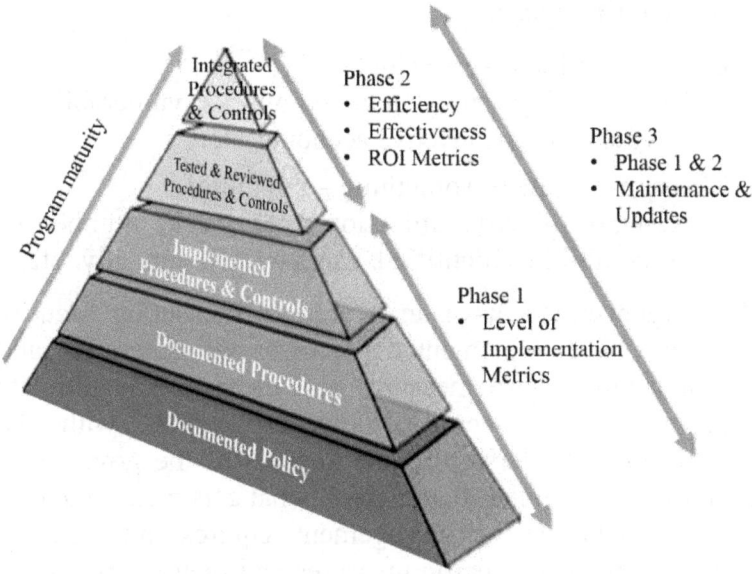

Figure 24: Phased approach to metrics

Every metric must be identified and linked to a specific security objective. Given the resources required, metrics and the associated data collection efforts should focus on using readily available sources to provide the necessary information. *Figure 25* illustrates this data identification, collection, storage, and analysis process.

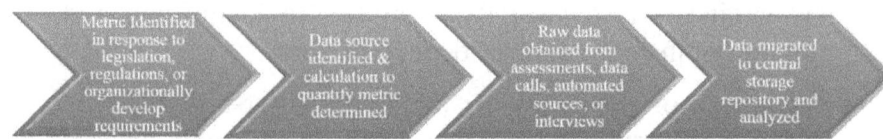

Figure 25: Data collection process

Most of the organizations will likely apply one of the typical metrics approaches:

- Count something – anything!
  - Number of systems, attempted attacks, vulnerabilities, privileged users, inactive accounts, etc.
- Measure the rate of something – anything!
  - Number of virus infections per week, number of vulnerabilities identified, users trained annually, etc.

Most organizations have an interest in measuring security value and have implemented processes for generating and communicating these measures and metrics. The ultimate responsibility for security, however, resides with the organizational leadership as the keepers of the governance framework. A popular dictum says 'what gets measured, gets done'. So when senior management requires and regularly receives reports of specific measures and metrics, personnel are quick to understand what is important to leadership.

It is the responsibility of the leadership and the organizational elements identified at the beginning of this section to identify, approve and articulate the set of metrics that best reflect an insider threat security program. *Figure 26* shows the most common types of measures collected and reported to organizational leadership.[108]

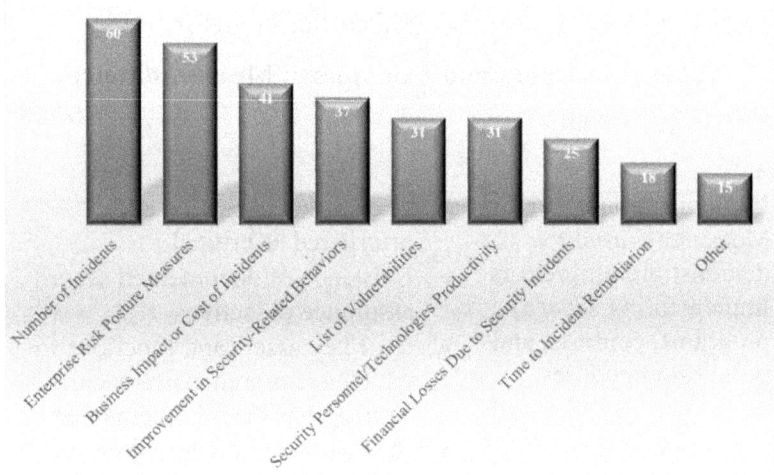

**Figure 26: Measures/metrics commonly reported
to management**

But in reality, these types of metrics do not really answer the questions 'Are we secure enough?' and 'How do I know what is secure, and how will I know if we're there?' The first and most important tip is to start small – identify a manageable set of security metrics. For each metric and measure identified, the following information at a minimum also needs to be developed: purpose, frequency of monitoring or data collection, implementation evidence, formula for analysis (if appropriate), and data source.

NIST Standard Publication 800-55, *Performance Measurement Guide for Information Security*, identifies three primary categories of measures and metrics.[109] For each category, examples of measures/metrics are provided. It is important to note that these are by no means all inclusive – an organization will have to determine which measures and metrics are most appropriate and which meet the metrics determination factors described earlier in this section.

Table 1: Category and Examples of Measures/Metrics

Category of Measures/ Metrics	Examples of Measures/Metrics
Implementation Measures – used to demonstrate progress in implementing security programs, controls, and policies/procedures	• % of assets identified and prioritized as critical • Existence of documented security assurance objectives • % of key assets and functions for which a comprehensive security strategy has been implemented • % of security requirements for which approved policies and controls have been implemented • % of key security management roles for which responsibility and authority have been assigned and skills identified • % of partner and other third-party relationships for which security requirements have been identified and implemented • % of job performance reviews that include evaluation of security responsibilities and security compliance • % of individuals whose access privileges have been reviewed and validated
Effectiveness/Efficiency Measures – used to determine whether processes and controls	• % of security incidents caused by improper access controls • Length of time required to react to an incident

Category of Measures/ Metrics	Examples of Measures/Metrics
have been implemented correctly, operate as intended, and achieve the intended outcome. They incorporate two aspects of control implementation: robustness of the result (e.g., effectiveness) and timeliness of the result (e.g., efficiency)	• % of security compliance reviews with limited or no findings • Length of time required to return to full operational capacity • % of security incidents that exploited existing vulnerabilities with known solutions • % of systems where audit logs and collected and regularly reviewed
Impact Measures – determine business or mission impact of security on the organization's ability to accomplish its mission	• Return on Investment (ROI) on security protections/countermeasures • Costs incurred as a result of security incidents • Degree of trust or reputation gained/lost • % of security incidents that did/did not cause damage, compromise assets or loss beyond established tolerance • Damage or loss in dollars resulting from security incidents

So what are the benefits, if any, of having a measurement program? The primary benefits are increased accountability for security performance, improved effectiveness of security activities, demonstrated compliance with laws, regulations, and policies, and quantifiable data to support resource allocation decisions.

To date, there are few, if any, measures and metrics specifically designed to address insider threat mitigation objectives. However, security metrics used to measure general program effectiveness can frequently be adapted to address insider threat concerns. More information on measures development, implementation, and analysis can be obtained from the resources listed below.

The Quick Wins

- Establish processes for metric collection using existing processes and automation, to the maximum extent possible.
- Capitalize on relationships with other elements within the organization to collect metrics; obtain buy-in from stakeholders.
- Establish benchmarks for identified objectives prior to initiating any collection; measure against the pre-determined benchmarks.
- Relate security metrics to the business and mission of the organization.
- Use results of metrics analysis to continuously improve the insider threat (InT) program.

Standards Mapping

STANDARD	CONTROL	SUBJECT
NIST 800-53, Rev 4, Security Controls for Federal Information Systems and Organizations	CA-7	Continuous Monitoring
NIST 800-55, Performance Measurement Guide for Information Security	3.0	Information Security Measures Background

STANDARD	CONTROL	SUBJECT
	5.0	Measures Development Process
	6.0	Information Security Measurement Implementation
ISO/IEC 27004:2009, Information Security – Security techniques – Information Security Management – Measurement	5	Information security measurement overview
	7	Measures and measurement development
	9	Data analysis and measurements results reporting

Recommendations for Additional Reading

Wong, Caroline. *Security Metrics, A Beginner's Guide.* November 2011. McGraw-Hill Education Publishing.

Jaquith, Andrew. *Security Metrics: Replacing Fear, Uncertainty and Doubt.* March 2007. Addison-Wesley Professional Publishing.

4. Apply Policy Levers and Controls

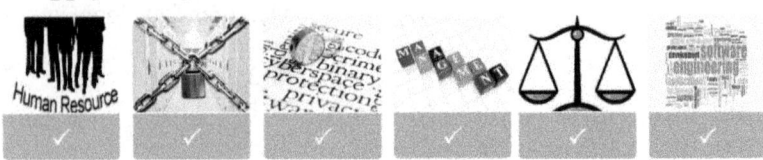

In order to deter, detect, and respond to attacks on information systems and information, organizations tend to rely on a number of applied administrative and technical security controls. The CMU SEI MERIT research reviewed several categories of these controls and identified the potential value of employing these measures. The table below provides a high-level review of these policy and technical controls, together with an analysis of the likelihood of success and inadvertent results.[110] While CMU SEI focused its research on IT, these generic policy levers and controls can be applied in other situations as well. They are listed in no particular order of priority.

Table 2: Policy Levers and Controls

Control	Description	Inadvertent Result
Sanctions	Punitive measures intended to motivate the employee to reduce or eliminate inappropriate personal or behavior.	May increase level of disgruntlement and inadvertently cause additional inappropriate behavior.
Intervention	Employee assistance or counselling focused on lowering levels of discontent	May be ineffective if quality of intervention is inadequate and timing

Control	Description	Inadvertent Result
	or to reduce improper behavior.	is sporadic.
Monitoring	Real-time tracking and analysis of an insider's actions.	If monitoring is inconsistent or quality is lacking, may not provide an adequate result.
Auditing	Discover, understand, review and disable any access paths available to the insider.	Poor auditing practices may allow insiders to identify efforts at tracking and use this to conceal actions.
Training	Education of employees on insider threat and appropriate usage of IT or protection of corporate resources.	May have little effect if of poor quality or sporadic delivery.
Reporting	Encouragement for employees to report security breaches or suspicious behavior.	Employees may fear punitive actions or they may not want to be seen as 'tattlers' who are not team players.

Despite some of the seemingly negative results, sound security policies and procedures that are implemented, emphasized, and followed may indeed resolve many of the insider threat challenges. In order to achieve these positive results, the policy must be clear, consistent, and fair – and any sanctions must be proportionate to the offense.

A further challenge is ensuring that the policy is communicated, understood and enforced. All too often employees take intellectual property developed in one job to another without realizing that this is a violation, on account of a lack of clear communication of expectations. One of the primary means to communicate this form of policy is to have the employee read and sign a comprehensive Non-Disclosure Agreement (NDA) and an Acceptable Use Policy (AUP). Each employee should be given a signed copy of each document and the organization should retain the signed originals as evidence that the individual has read and agreed to the conditions stated in the documents.

The purpose of an AUP is to clearly outline the proper and authorized use of the organization's information and information systems. It can protect the employee as well as the organization, from risks stemming from inappropriate use or malicious activity. Be sure that every employee understands the AUP and the sanctions that will be applied if the policy is violated.

An NDA is a formal confidentiality agreement that creates a legal obligation for an employee to protect any intellectual property or other organizational confidential information. Most importantly, in terms of insider threat, a signed NDA provides legal recourse for damages incurred if that information is improperly taken and disclosed. In order to be effective, an NDA must include clear descriptions of the assets to be protected and any exclusions, the obligation of the employee to protect the information assets, the time frame for which the NDA is valid, and the sanctions for violation.

While communication is one side of the challenge, the other is documentation. Clear documentation of policies and controls can prevent employee misunderstandings and ensure that employees feel as if they are all treated equally. Written policies and controls should be clear and concise. The US military writing guide provides some guidance in writing for a large, diverse audience:

- Write clear and logical sentences which expresses an idea in as few words as possible;
- Choose effective words and phrases;
- Use concrete words and avoid abstract concepts;
- Keep the language simple and avoid 'gobbledygook'*;
- Use action words and avoid the passive voice.

In fact, one US Army regulation says that the average sentence should be no longer than 15 words and that each word should ideally be no more than two syllables. Finally, a policy should put the bottom line up front. When I was a fresh US Government employee, I wrote a long research paper. I was working for a three-star general at the time and I was incensed when the paper was returned to me with the letters BLUF written in red across the top. To my great embarrassment, I confronted the general saying: "My research is valid, it is not a bluff." He then told me that BLUF meant 'bottom line up front' – I should always open with what's most important and what I want the reader to take away as the main point. It was a valuable lesson.

---

* The Military Writing Guide defines gobbledygook as (a) using 100 words to say what could be said in 20, (b) using words that are unfamiliar, (c) using words of three or four syllables when simpler words could convey the same idea, (d) incorporating jargon or overworked phrases, and (e) using long and involved sentences.

There are two very important notes regarding policy. First, you can't hold someone accountable for what they don't know or haven't been told. Each individual joining, or working for, the organization should receive a copy of the policies. The organization should retain proof that the individual has read, understood, and consented to the policy requirements. This is often referred to as the Acceptable Use Policy (AUP).

System administrators and others with elevated privileges present a unique challenge and potential danger to an organization. In addition to the AUP, privileged users should read and sign a Privileged Use Agreement (PUA), which defines the special requirements for users with privileged accesses.

It is also mandatory that management not be exempt from compliance with policies and procedures. One of the recurring factors motivating insider threats is the perception of inequality or unmet expectations. If managers are not held to the same standard as other employees, it will be noted and potentially lead to the perception that management does not stand behind its own policies and procedures.

Secondly, any security policy that is not enforced will quickly be ignored. If penalties are employed whenever policies are violated, individuals in the organization will soon recognize that negative behaviors are penalized. The consequences of not meting out appropriate and rapid punitive measures for violations of the organization's fundamental security principles is this: employees who are prone to violations will continue to commit them with impunity.

The Quick Wins

- Ensure that management supports, enforces and – most importantly – complies with organizational policies and procedures.
- Ensure that policy levers and controls are consistently applied without the appearance of favoritism or prejudice.

Standards Mapping

STANDARD	CONTROL	SUBJECT
NIST 800-53, Security Controls for Federal Information Systems and Organizations	PL-1	Security Planning Policy and Procedures
	PL-4	Rules of Behavior
	PS-8	Personnel Sanctions
ISO/IEC 27001:2013, Information technology – Security techniques – Information Security Management Systems – Requirements	A.5.1	Information security policy
	A.5.1.1	Information security policy document
	A.5.1.2	Review of the information security policy
	A.15.1	Compliance with legal requirements
	A.15.1.1	Identification of applicable legislation
ISO/IEC 27002: 2013, Information technology – Security techniques – Code of practice for information security	5	Information security policies

STANDARD	CONTROL	SUBJECT
management		
	5.1	Management direction for information security
	5.1.1	Policies for information security
	5.1.2	Review of the policies for information security
	6	Organization of information security
	12.1	Operational procedures and responsibilities
	18.1.1	Identification of applicable legislation and contractual requirements

Recommendations for Additional Reading
Security Policy Research: The Insider Threat – Security Policies to Reduce Risk. 2011. Information Shield, Inc. Link: *www.informationshield.com/papers/Security%20 Policies%20Address%20the%20Insider%20Threat.pdf*
U.S. National Insider Threat Policy and Minimum Standards for Executive Branch Insider Threat Programs. November 2012. *www.gpo.gov/fdsys/pkg/ DCPD-201200905/content-detail.html*

5. Create a Culture of Security

 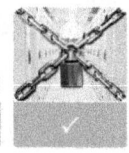    

Why do some security and insider threat initiatives succeed, while others fail miserably? The solution may lie within the organizational culture. So, what is that? A corporate culture is the invisible core comprised of the values, priorities, objectives, and assumptions of those within the organization. Just as the human body will reject a foreign object, the most well-thought out security initiative may fail because of an incompatibility with the overall organizational culture.

Every organization has an overall culture, and the security culture for each organization must be as unique as the organization itself. Creating a culture of security may sound like a simple act, but it requires both leadership and extensive employee participation, as well as a clear understanding of both the overall corporate culture and the requirement for security.

Edgar H. Schein, a professor of management at the Massachusetts Institute of Technology (MIT), outlined a three-tier method for understanding and defining a corporate culture. These three levels are depicted in *Figure 27*, and begin with artifacts, move through values, and conclude with shared assumptions.[111]

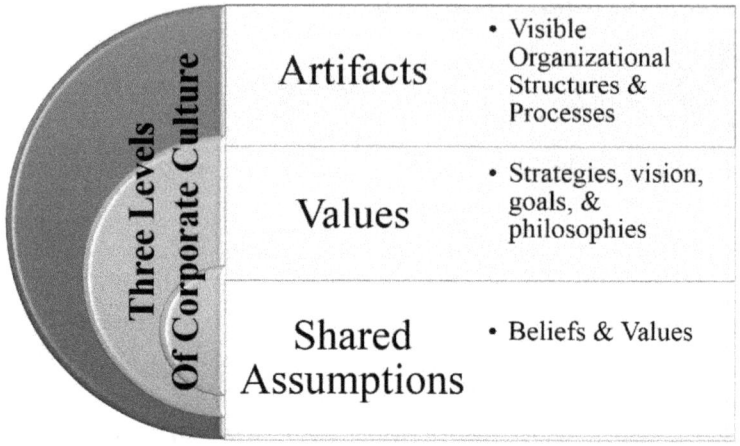

Figure 27: Edgar Stein's three levels of corporate culture

The items identified at the Artifacts level of the corporate culture include a number that may not be immediately noticeable, but which together comprise the organizations common processes; for example, normal working hours, dress code, office layout, corporate hierarchy, support for work/life balance and formality/informality of communications. *Figure 28* shows how these artifacts are pieces of the corporate culture puzzle.

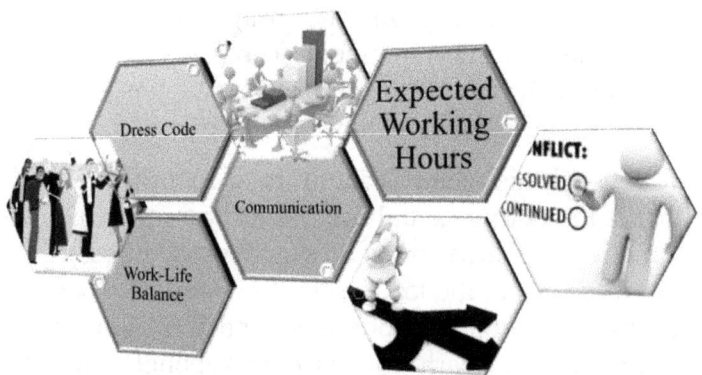

Graphics Source: Freestockimages.com

Figure 28: Pieces of the corporate culture puzzle (adapted from Edgar H. Schein)

At the Values level, the organization clarifies how cultural values affect the Artifact level. This level can be addressed in a number of dimensions, such as the corporate philosophy on work ethic. For example, many technology companies today equate number of hours spent at work with loyalty to the company and the team. Other companies may focus on encouraging work-life balance as part of their corporate ethic. Some organizations may have a relatively flat hierarchy and place a high value on open and informal communications. More traditional organizations, such as financial institutions or government agencies, may have a strict hierarchy and associated expectations of more formal communications lines.

The final level, Shared Assumptions, focuses on those elements of the culture that are considered concrete. These assumptions influence the experiential values that drive decision making within the organization. It is at this level that employees are acclimated to the tacit or visible corporate culture, much in the way individuals are socialized within their environment. Those readers who are *Star Trek* fans will remember the chant: "We are the Borg. You will be assimilated. Resistance is futile."[112]

So, how does all this relate to a culture of security? I would argue that if the corporate culture has artifacts that indicate institutionalized security processes and procedures, if the corporate values from the leadership down reflect a position that security is of utmost importance, and if all individuals in the organization learn to share this belief, then the organization may have been successful in creating a culture of security. The primary factor for participation is a sense of responsibility for security and a feeling of ownership.

An element of corporate culture critical to addressing the ever-evolving insider threat is innovation. A security-oriented culture is highly dependent upon creativity and innovation to combat the equally creative individuals with malicious intent. Insider threats can be very creative in exploiting weaknesses; thwarting them demands the same inventiveness as the potential threat. A related element is the ability to adapt the organization to a changing environment. Increased use of social media and new technologies, such as the Cloud, require changes to regulatory requirements, policies and procedures.

The Quick Wins

- A security-oriented culture begins at the top. Ensure that leadership demonstrates the desired culture of security values.

- Establish the roles and responsibilities essential to creating a culture of security and assign them to individuals who will be given both responsibility and authority.

- Create and implement a security training program that incorporates and teaches the elements of the organization's security culture.

- Ensure corporate security policies are easily accessible and that the related security procedures are published and followed. Establish a recognition program for security innovation.

- Ensure leadership, management, and co-workers use communication as a tool for creating a successful culture of security. Take the time to explain why certain practices are required.

- Periodically re-assess security policies to ensure that they are keeping pace with ongoing trends and organization change and growth.

Standards Mapping

STANDARD	CONTROL	SUBJECT
NIST 800-53, Security Controls for Federal Information Systems and Organizations	PL-4	Rules of Behavior
	PM-11	Mission/Business Process Definition
	SA-2	Allocation of Resources
ISO/IEC 27001:2013, Information technology – Security techniques – Information Security Management Systems – Requirements	A.6.1.1	Management commitment to information security
	A.6.1.2	Information security

STANDARD	CONTROL	SUBJECT
		coordination
	A.6.1.3	Allocation of information security responsibilities
ISO/IEC 27002: 2013, Information technology – Security techniques – Code of practice for information security management	6.1	Internal organization

Recommendations for Additional Reading
Roer, Kai. *Build a Security Culture*. March 2015. IT Governance Publishing. Cambridgeshire, U.K.
Zakaria, Omar. *Information Security Culture: A Human Firewall Approach*. May 2013. LAP Lambert Academic Publishing.

6. Anticipate and Prepare for Negative Events

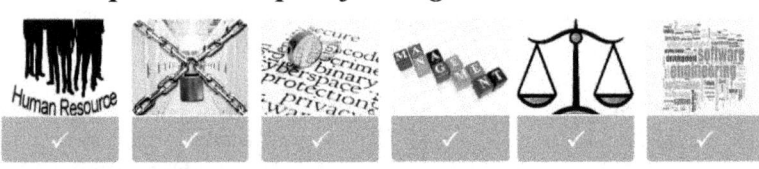

The ability to anticipate and prepare for insider threat events is directly related to the implementation of the insider threat program and the creation of an organization-wide culture of security. Equally important is the perception that the existing policies and requirements are equitably and consistently enforced. This is particularly critical, since many of the historical insider threat cases were motivated by perceived inequities or injustices.

Organizations need to be sensitive to certain events that can trigger the perception of privileged treatment, or to a sensitivity to unmet expectations. Examples of these situations were provided in the CMU SEI Common Sense Guide to Mitigating Insider Threats. It is common for employees to look forward to the annual performance evaluation period, which is frequently associated with promotions and/or raises in salary. Some companies have established a culture over time where such recognition has become commonplace and employees have come to expect the same level of reward every year. When this does not occur – for whatever reason – some employees may feel cheated and become disgruntled. One way of anticipating and preparing for this possible situation is for the company to inform their employees of the changes as soon as possible, provide the rationale (e.g., temporary heightened financial uncertainty), and look for alternative means of recognition.

A similar situation might occur when organizations are being 'flattened' or a company has lost a critical contract and may have to release employees. In 2013-2014, the US officially announced the end of the 'War on Terror' and indicated that all of the Department of Defense organizations and the Services (e.g., Army, Navy, Air Force) would be exposed to accelerated budget reductions and associated force drawdown. This announcement was accompanied by a personnel tumult, since a drawdown generally involves separation for military careerists and involuntary reduction in the civilian workforce supporting the military organizations. In this situation, the US Department of Defense needed a heightened sensitivity to any unusual behavior, and should have implemented measures to head off any potential insider threat activity.

In any organization, there will be times when employees will seek assistance for issues either within the workplace or in their outside life. Perhaps they are having challenges with a co-worker and feel like they are in a hostile work environment. Or an employee may be experiencing significant financial difficulties because of a life event outside of work. In these cases, if an employee approaches their organization for assistance and understanding, there is an expectation that they will be taken seriously and their issue can be discussed without fear of reprisal – or without fear that their discussions will not be treated confidentially. A formal reporting mechanism and a trained assistance staff (in HR, for example) can go far in assisting the organization in the early identification and mitigation of potential insider threats.

The Quick Wins

- Be aware of any situations that might result in unfulfilled expectations and employee disgruntlement and 'head them off at the pass'.
- Ensure leadership regularly and clearly communicates any changes to the members and associates of the organization.
- Establish and publish employee reporting channels and ensure assistants are trained in how to handle employee reports in a trusted, confidential and equitable manner.

Standards Mapping

STANDARD	CONTROL	SUBJECT
NIST 800-53, Security Controls for Federal Information Systems and Organizations	PL-4	Rules of Behavior
	PS-6	Access Agreements
	PS-8	Personnel Sanctions
ISO/IEC 27001:2013, Information technology – Security techniques – Information Security Management Systems – Requirements	A.8.1.3	Terms and conditions of employment
	A.8.2.3	Disciplinary process
	A.10.2.2	Monitoring and review of third party services
ISO/IEC 27002: 2013, Information technology – Security techniques – Code of practice for information security management	7	Human resource security
	15.1.2	Addressing security within supplier agreements
	16.1.6	Learning from information security incidents

Recommendations for Additional Reading

McMillan, Rob. *Prepare for the Inevitable with an Effective Security Incident Response Plan.* 19 July 2012. Available at Gartner Research: *www.gartner.com/doc/ 2086516/prepare-inevitable-effective-security-incident*

Training and Awareness

7. Ensure All Employees Receive Initial and Periodic Insider Threat Recognition Training

 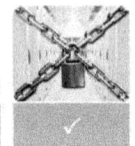    

Of all the best practices, the greatest near-term payoff may be in establishing a robust security awareness, training, and education program. In many cases the workforce has no appreciation or understanding of insider threat, or they may think 'it can't happen here'. Every employee or business partner, contractor or consultant must understand that insider threats do happen and can have grave consequences. Equally important is the knowledge that an Insider does not carry a sign or any other form of identification. They look just like anyone else. They do not necessarily fit a specific profile. "The CERT Insider Threat Center's collection of insider threat cases reveals a wide range of people who have committed crimes, from low-wage earners to executives, and new hires to seasoned company veterans."[113]

But there are ways to recognize certain higher risk individuals and to implement mitigating strategies to reduce their impact. One of the best ways to impart this knowledge to the organization is through initial training and regular refresher courses.

Successful training focuses on creating a culture of security. At a minimum, insider threat training should provide knowledge of:

- motivation, characteristics, and behavioral precursors of insider threat;

- technical aspects of insider fraud, theft of IP, or sabotage;
- observables to look for within the organization that could signal a pending insider attack;
- reporting procedures for security violations;
- actionable steps that can be taken to better manage insider threat risk in the organization;
- organizational cybersecurity policy and procedures;
- acceptable use policies and expectations;
- best practices that can mitigate, or even prevent, insider incidents.

Insider threat training should be based on the documented policies and procedures. Employees should understand that insider threat mitigation is based on established policies and procedures, not on arbitrary judgement, and that managers will not 'shoot the messenger.' This enables employees to report suspicious behaviors without fear of retribution and helps to defeat the cultural barriers to whistleblowing or 'snitching'.

All of the departments noted above should participate in the development and even the delivery of the training. HR can discuss the personnel issues associated with insider threat. Legal can provide the legislative and regulatory requirements. Physical and facilities security should review access policies and procedures. Management and information owners may highlight the importance of increased awareness of insider threat and which assets are of great importance to protect. Information about the dangers of malware and phishing can be the contribution of the IT and cybersecurity staff, while the IT engineering staff can discuss the importance of configuration management and good security engineering.

In addition to organizationally-delivered training, there are other sources of insider threat training. For example, the US Defense Security Service (DSS) has established a series of courses focused on Insider Threat Awareness and Training, most of which are openly available. This training is part of an Insider Threat Toolkit and can be found at *www.cdse.edu/toolkits/insider/awareness.html*.

The Quick Wins

- Train all incoming employees and other consultants, contractors, and partners in security awareness prior to allowing them access to any information system. Ensure this training includes awareness of insider threat.

- Conduct security training continuously – it's not 'one and done'. The training can take many forms, including newsletters, informative emails, and screensavers.

- Ensure the training program has visible management support and active participation.

- Establish a security incident reporting mechanism that is both anonymous and simple.

Standards Mapping

STANDARD	CONTROL	SUBJECT
NIST 800-53, Security Controls for Federal Information Systems and Organizations	AT-1	Awareness and Training Policy and Procedures
	AT-2	Security Awareness Training
	AT-3	Role-Based Security Training

STANDARD	CONTROL	SUBJECT
ISO/IEC 27001:2013, Information technology – Security techniques – Information Security Management Systems-Requirements	7.3	Awareness
ISO/IEC 27002:2013, Information technology – Security techniques – Code of practice for information security management	8.2.2	Information security awareness, education, and training

Recommendations for Additional Reading
Insider Threat Toolkit: Awareness and Training. Link: *www.cdse.edu/toolkits/insider/awareness.html*
Maddock, Valerie. *IT Induction and Information Security Awareness*. 9 February 2010. IT Governance Publishing.

Personnel Security and Management

8. Conduct Background Screenings

Training and awareness can be effective ways to help employees identify and deter potential insider threat activities. Organizations are realizing that it is preferable to spot a potential insider threat *before* they join the organization. One way to do this is to establish a process for employee vetting or background screening.

All individuals in an organization, but especially those requiring any form of privileged access, should be required to undergo a vetting process, most often known as background screening. The level of background screening should be commensurate with the level of privilege and access required by the individual and the sensitivity of the functions they perform. Background screening has long been an element within US Government agencies and the financial sector. However, "According to Chantelle Norman, head of business development for Kroll Background Worldwide Ltd., pre-employment vetting has been slow to take off in the UK."[114]

While background screenings are not foolproof, the lack of a screening of sufficient depth could leave the organization vulnerable to individuals being placed in critical positions without sufficient trustworthiness for the level of access and privilege required. Certainly, background screenings cannot provide a guarantee of an individual's future honesty, but they can mitigate the risk. In fact, Snowden's insider threat activities have focused a laser-like level of attention on deficiencies in the US Government's background screening processes. Since many private sector screening processes are loosely based on public sector practices, it is reasonable to assume that there are also significant gaps in the corporate environment.

The background screening process should be designed to detect potential risk factors, such as previous negative behaviors, criminal convictions, suspicious contacts, addictions, financial difficulties, etc. The screening should also verify previous employment and credentials. Here's a real-life example of how the lack of in-depth background screening can go very awry. The Information Security Officer (ISO) in an unnamed organization departed his position quietly and quickly after being employed for more than a year. One day, shortly after the organization instituted a more formal process for employee screening – beginning with current employees and extending to prospective employees – the newly-employed background check process revealed that the ISO was on probation for felony embezzlement. In fact, he had been released from prison only a short time before being hired by the organization. *Until that point, the company was completely unaware that the ISO had legal problems.* In the case of this ISO, it turned out that HR had been in a hurry to hire an individual to fill a critical position and had neglected to perform any background checks.

Prior to conducting any background screenings, the organization must consult with legal counsel familiar with the local, state, and national regulations and restrictions. In most cases, the content of the background screenings must be limited to job-related requirements and respect the local and national privacy laws. Control A.7.1.1, of ISO/IEC 27001 specifies: "Background verification checks on all candidates from employment shall be carried out in accordance with relevant laws, regulations and ethics, and proportional to business requirements, the classification of the information to be accessed, and the perceived risks."[115]

Note that organizations need to look at each individual holistically. "We advise our clients to look at the whole picture, because so many people have credit problems at the moment, and if someone is trying to pay back their debts, then they may well be a loyal and hardworking employee. Similarly, a criminal record for a teenage misdemeanor may have little bearing on the trustworthiness of a thirty-something candidate."[116]

Most organizations tend to restrict background screenings to their direct employees. Good practice is to extend these screenings to contractors and their subcontractors, consultants, and other individuals providing services to the organization.

The Quick Wins

- Ensure all employees, contractors, consultants, service providers and business partners have undergone a background screening at the appropriate level based on their function and access.
- Ensure all screenings include a criminal background and financial check at a minimum.
- If necessary, hire an outside service specializing in conducting employee background screenings.

Standards Mapping

STANDARD	CONTROL	SUBJECT
NIST 800-53, Security Controls for Federal Information Systems and Organizations	PS-2	Position Risk Designation
	PS-3	Personnel Screening
ISO/IEC 27001:2013, Information technology – Security techniques – Information Security Management Systems – Requirements	A.8.1.2	Screening
ISO/IEC 27002:2013, Information technology – Security techniques – Code of practice for	8.1.2	Screening

STANDARD	CONTROL	SUBJECT
information security management		

Recommendations for Additional Reading
Blackwell, Clive. *The Insider Threat: A Pocket Guide*. April 2007. IT Governance Publishing, Cambridgeshire, UK.

9. Establish a Baseline for Normal User Behavior

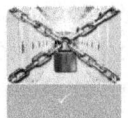

With the exception of the CMU SEI, very few organizations are likely to have an integrated database of insider case studies, lessons learned, psychological profiles, or insider threat statistics. Nor should they.

However, every organization could potentially obtain benefits from establishing an informal profile of insider threat behavior indicators. Insider threat indicators, in many cases, are not all that different from other outward manifestations of betrayal of trust. "The act of conducting an insider attack carries with it cognitive and social challenges that may affect an offender's day-to-day work behavior."[117]

The first step in identifying anomalous behaviors is to determine a baseline for normal or expected patterns of behavior based on role within the organization. For example, a simple user's standard patterns of system usage would be considerably different from that of a privileged user. A manager's physical or digital access baseline would be different from that of a general employee. A financial institution with a risk-averse culture would have a very different set of expected behaviors than a modern technology company with its environment based on innovation and sharing. It is incumbent on each organization to examine its own culture and characteristics in order to form an expected behavior profile. *Chapter 2* outlines a number of behavioral characteristics and patterns that could point to a potential insider threat.

Research by Taylor, et. al., indicates that language usage and changes over time might provide one method of identifying the potential – or even active – insider threat. Considering that verbal and written expression is a reflection of an individual's state of mind, certain changes to language might reveal an insider threat's mental state. The benefit of observing and analyzing linguistic changes is that it can often be done unobtrusively and without attracting undue attention either from the possible insider threat or from others within the organization.

CMU SEI[118] studies have indicated that many insider threats were characterized by an increased focus on personal recognition and success over the collective goals of the organization. They were also much less concerned with gaining and maintaining positive work relationships with their co-workers. Taylor, et.al. revealed that these changes in work perspective and co-worker relationships could be reflected linguistically through an increased use of first-person singular and second person pronouns. This may often be linked with "heightened negative affect and expression of feelings compared to co-workers."[119]

Insider threats may also be burdened with the knowledge of their deception – most of us are aware that living with lies can cause stress. Taylor, et.al. found that the effort required by the insider threat to maintain a trustworthy appearance is associated with an inappropriate effort to appear open, while at the same time using circumspect language to avoid saying anything that might arouse the suspicion of co-workers or supervisors. "Liars used more tentative words than truth-tellers probably because they sought to avoid committing to a concrete version of their story."[120] Examples of this might be an increase in statements beginning with "I know this looks suspicious, but..." or "Perhaps my actions should have been..."

One important aspect of Taylor's research is the emphasis on the need to identify insider threats early, since it appears that the insider may adapt to the deceitful nature of their situation over time and their behavior may begin to normalize.

Insider threats may also display a tendency to distance themselves from others. This can be reflected in fewer or shorter communications or in the act of seeking physical separation.

If an employee's behavior becomes suspicious, it is extremely important that an organization act with due care. While most of the best practices emphasize procedures and processes that are clear in their application, this particular best practice must be exercised with caution and consideration. Over the course of employment, individuals may often encounter life events that may temporarily or even permanently affect their behavior – and these may not necessarily indicate that the individual has suddenly become an insider threat. In many cases of anomalous behavior, the organization may actually aid the individual by providing options to help them cope, such as referral to an anonymous employee assistance program.

The Quick Wins

- Establish an anonymous employee reporting system, such as a tip line, to encourage workers to report concerns about another employee's behavior.

- Investigate and document any incidences of behavior that deviates from the expected norms or that has one or more elements of the characteristics or patterns of an insider threat.

- Invest time and resources in training supervisors, managers, and co-workers to recognize and respond to inappropriate or concerning behaviors.

- Establish an anonymous employee assistance program to help employees dealing with life-changing events.

Standards Mapping

STANDARD	CONTROL	SUBJECT
NIST 800-53, Security Controls for Federal Information Systems and Organizations	PS-1	Personnel Security Policy and Procedures
ISO/IEC 27002:2013, Information technology – Security techniques – Code of practice for information security management	7.2	Emphasize security during employment
ISO/IEC 27001:2013, Information technology– Security techniques –	A.7.1.1	Screening

STANDARD	CONTROL	SUBJECT
Information security management systems – Requirements		
	A.7.2.3	Disciplinary Process

Recommendations for Additional Reading
Puleo, Anthony J. *Mitigating Insider Threat Using Human Behavior Influence Models.* October 2012. BiblioScholar Publications.

10. Monitor and Quickly Respond to Suspicious Behaviors

 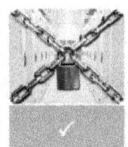   

After-the-fact studies of actual insider threats reveal that managers and co-workers often observed some of the tell-tale behavioral signs, but rarely raised the alarm. One of the benefits to developing a model for normal user behavior is the ability to detect deviations. Once this model is developed, supervisors and workers must be made aware of this model and the path for reporting unusual behavioral manifestations.

There are privacy/ethical issues in monitoring employee and business partner behaviors. This process must be implemented with great care in order to avoid a perception that employees are under undue scrutiny and that any unusual behavior could potentially result in negative consequences. At any given time, life stresses can cause an otherwise normal individual to exhibit uncharacteristic traits – the trick is to understand that insider threat behaviors will occur over time with a certain degree of consistency.

Additionally, supervisors and co-workers should be trained to discern between acts that occur through malice and intent and those that are the result of an intentional or unintentional disregard for security policies.

Beginning with the initial employment process, organizations must devise an approach to dealing with the potential for insider threat. Among the tools available to employers are background checks, which should include a credit check, scans for criminal convictions, verification of credentials, and discussions with previous employers.

Outside of organizations requiring specialized security clearances – such as defense and government organizations – or bonding, such as financial and health providers – most employees will only be subject to background reviews during the hiring process.

Individuals who can control or influence organizational assets, or who have access to proprietary information and/or information system administrative functions, demand a higher level of assurance in their trustworthiness, reliability and loyalty. Despite this, most organizations only require those with enhanced access or privileges to undergo the same vetting procedures as other employees or partners.

In addition to an initial background check, each organization should develop a mix of investigative, adjudicative, and employee behavior monitoring methods to maintain an acceptable level of assurance. Security is better served if the organization has a process for continual online review of personal information. Data mining, such as reviews of social media activities, can provide essential indicators of malicious insider behavior that might otherwise to unheeded.

Prior to initiating any background reviews or online monitoring, it is critical to obtain legal guidance on national, state and local regulations may limit the use of monitoring or certain checks. Information obtained from background checks and monitoring is protected under the relevant privacy laws and should only be used properly, with due consideration to the nature and duration of the information. It should only be accessed as one component of a risk-based decision to allow an individual to view critical assets or confidential or proprietary information. This is a sensitive area and legal counsel must be obtained to ensure all monitoring activities are within the bounds of law. Some areas that are generally excluded are:

- Private communications between the individual and their legal representative or medical providers.
- 'Whistleblower'* communications that are considered protected disclosures.

One of the primary means to recognize the potential insider threat is to identify those actions in advance that could be indicators of inappropriate behavior and to make a list of these available. Supervisors are in a position to notice such behaviors, but they often do not act if the behavior is not a

---

* 'Whistleblower' refers to information, usually confidential, provided by an employee regarding waste, fraud, abuse or corruption.

specific violation of policy. It is a worthwhile investment to train supervisors to recognize – but most importantly to respond to – behavioral indicators.

One of the most prominent and consistent indicators may be an employee's or partner's financial problems or even unexplained financial gains. Research by both CMU SEI and CIFAS indicates that financial motives were the most common sources of fraudulent activity, such as identify theft or credit card fraud. If sudden changes in an individuals' financial status are noted, such as increased debt or uncharacteristically expensive purchases, these could be signs of potential insider threat.

There are certainly some legal, as well as ethical, concerns regarding employee monitoring. These challenges include:

- legal limitations to sharing information with those responsible for protecting the organization;
- conveying a sense of "big brother" watching over individual actions, which can affect morale and productivity;
- ensuring that only legally allowable communications or online presence is monitored;
- legal restrictions to using arrest or conviction records when making decisions on hiring, promoting, demoting or transferring an employee.

It is important to note that legal limitations and restrictions may vary according to location. This book is written largely from the perspective of US law, which may also vary from state to state. It is imperative for any organization to understand the legal requirements within its own area of operation.

The Quick Wins

- Establish personnel security vetting procedures commensurate with each individual's level of access or privileges.

- Identify positions that require a greater level of trust and ensure individuals applying for these positions are more thoroughly investigated and monitored.

- Identify insider threat indicators and train employees and supervisors on inappropriate behavior or insider threat signals.

- Establish confidential reporting channels and procedures.

Standards Mapping

STANDARD	CONTROL	SUBJECT
NIST 800-53, Security Controls for Federal Information Systems and Organizations	PS-1	Personnel Security Policy and Procedures
	PS-2	Position Risk Designation
	PS-3	Personnel Screening
	PS-8	Personnel Sanctions
ISO/IEC 27001:2013, Information technology – Security techniques – Information security management systems – Requirements	A.7.1.1	Screening
	A.7.2.3	Disciplinary Process
ISO/IEC 27002:2013, Information technology – Security techniques – Code of practice for	7.1	Emphasize security prior to employment

STANDARD	CONTROL	SUBJECT
information security management		
	7.2	Emphasize security during employment

Recommendations for Additional Reading
Stanton, Jeffrey M. and Stam, Kathryn R. *The Visible Employee: Using Workplace Monitoring and Surveillance to Protect Information Assets – Without Compromising Employee Privacy or Trust.* June 2006. Information Today, Inc.

11. Manage and Monitor Social Media Use by Employees

Existing, emerging, and not-yet-developed social media applications are changing the business world. Social media and its increasing adoption, particularly among certain demographics, poses a unique threat in terms of the insider. Social media applications include such sites as Facebook, Pinterest, Tumblr, YouTube, Twitter, Flickr, WordPress, and many, many more.

When paired with all the various types of mobile computing devices, social media takes on a new attack vector. "Whereas traditional battle space attack vectors have evolved over thousands of years, social media attack vectors have evolved rapidly creating challenges for those responsible with the defense of information and communications technology (ICT) systems and data."[121] Just think about this: email is about 40 years old and it took until 2009 to arrive at approximately 1.9 billion people worldwide who used email to communicate. Compare this to Facebook – Facebook was launched in 2004 and already has over 1 billion active users.[122]

Social media use has exploded and it seems as if a new social media site or app* is added every day. Certainly, organizations will find it difficult to monitor all of the possible social media communications. On which one(s) should an organization place its focus? Is it Facebook, Twitter, Flickr, YouTube – or all of the above? *Figure 29* only touches on all of the available options for social media use.

---

* The term "app" is the abbreviation for application. In terms of mobile devices, it refers to a program specifically designed for the mobile environment. iPhone first used the term in a commercial with the phrase "There's an app for that."

Figure 29: Social media sites and apps

Many individuals have written on the pros and cons of the social media explosion. John Mariotti, CEO and President of The Enterprise Group, had several – still valid – observations on the concerns regarding the proliferation of social media:

- At best, social media is an invitation to permanent and unrestrained overexposure, and at worst, an avenue for identity theft or misuse of personal information.

- The Internet environment is complex enough, but the uncontrolled proliferation of social media sites and apps adds an order of magnitude to the complexity.

- Social networking is still evolving and many of the social media sites and apps will either change or disappear.

- The security of social media sites and apps is still in a nascent phase. No matter how much one of these providers says personal information is protected, there is always the small print that gives these sites significant latitude in using the information placed on the sites.[123]

With social media frameworks available via the Internet, and with increasing number of employees accessing their Facebook or LinkedIn sites during work hours, the separation between leisure and work activities has become blurred. "What may seem like a simple social media interaction can reveal a lot about an individual or an organization."[124] In a recent study by SilkRoad, 'Social Media and Workplace Collaboration', SilkRoad identified that at least 75% of workers access their social media sites at least once per day while at work. There are several factors influencing this:

- Demographics in the workplace are changing, with an increasing number of new employees in the below-30 age range. This demographic is more likely to use social media, to use it more frequently, and to ignore their organization's IT policies and install social media tools on their work computers or phones.

- Organizations, even those that are in more conservative business sectors, such as finance or government, are embracing the collaborative benefits of social media.

- Increasing numbers of employers are using social media to screen and recruit candidates and for marketing purposes.

Organizational culture also plays a role in the degree of social media usage in the workplace. Organizations are increasingly accepting of a more transitory work force. This could be assessed as a sign that workplace loyalty, particularly in the form of long-term employment, is no longer valued or even expected. Generation Y and the Millennials are replacing the departing Baby Boomer Generation in the workforce, which is evolving relationships: loyalty is increasingly viewed as a reciprocal exchange, where loyalty from the individual is contingent upon loyalty from the organization.

The sector in which a company works also has an impact – technology-oriented companies are likely to see the benefits of incorporating social media into their business models, among others. Another influence on the use of social media is the national culture. Asian nations have a much higher percentage of social media use than the US or Europe. Bottom line, social media has become a part of the accepted social fabric and its use is now as mainstream today as using a landline phone was 20 years ago. Just as rules were established for monitoring phones, while taking expectations of privacy into account, so must there be rules for the monitoring of social media. If the main concern is about employees saying things they should not say, there is great benefit in teaching them what is off-limits and why this is critical to the company or its members. In other words, help the company members and affiliates to develop the knowledge and understanding they need to make good social media decisions, because once sensitive information has been posted to a social media site, the cat is out of the bag – and is already spitting up information hairballs all over the Internet.

But beyond concerns about the release of sensitive information by employees or affiliates, there has been a much more serious evolution in the use of social media. In a 2015 meeting between President Obama and UK Prime Minister Cameron, the President stated: "Social media and the Internet is the primary way in which terrorism organizations are communicating."[125] The terrorist group ISIS has clearly grasped the effectiveness of social media for forwarding its agenda. On August 19, 2014, ISIS used a YouTube video to show a graphic view of the beheading of

American journalist James Foley. This was followed by a release of additional videos and tweets announcing the beheading of four more individuals, American and British. These acts created a social media tsunami of negative reactions, but also stimulated a massive social media recruiting effort.

The December terrorist incident in San Bernardino illustrated that even the most non-threatening organizations can be hit by terrorists. After this incident, which involved a shooting at a holiday party for day care workers, FBI investigators revealed that Tashfeed Malik had posted private messages on Facebook that pledged support for Islamic jihad. A week before the attack, Malik left a Facebook post under an alias that included a pledge of allegiance to the leader of ISIS. The discovery of these posts revealed that law enforcement and intelligence officials has missed warnings on social media that Malik was a potential insider threat before she applied for and received her US visa. While this may be the darkest use of social media, and while most other social media activities will be much more benign, organizations can no longer ignore the potential for dangerous and potentially life-threatening social media activity.

The Quick Wins

- Develop and implement a social media policy which guides employees with respect to the proper and acceptable use of social media.

- Ensure policies clearly articulate the legitimate business use of social media, provide clear definitions of prohibited conduct, and specify the consequences for violations of the policy. Periodically review policies and procedures to ensure that the organization is effectively managing social media in a changing environment.

- Identify social media use that can be legally monitored or tracked to reasonably ensure compliance with corporate policies and procedures.

- If using social media to screen prospective employees and/or to monitor the activities of existing employees, obtain legal counsel. Aim to strike a legally-viable balance between monitoring employee activity and respecting employee legal privacy rights.

- Include appropriate use of social media in the organization's formal security training program.

Standards Mapping

STANDARD	CONTROL	SUBJECT
NIST 800-53, Security Controls for Federal Information Systems and Organizations	PL-4(1)	Rules of Behavior: Social Media and Networking Restrictions
ISO/IEC 27001:2013, Information technology – Security techniques – Information Security Management Systems – Requirements	6.2.1	Identification of risks related to external parties
	8.1.3	Terms and conditions of employment

Recommendations for Additional Reading
Lenkart, John J. *The Vulnerability of Social Networking Media and the Insider Threat: New Eyes for Bad Guys.*

February 2012. Naval Postgraduate School.

Social Media Governance Toolkit. Office 2010. 17 June 2010. IT Governance Publishing.

12. Enforce Separation of Duties and Least Privilege

 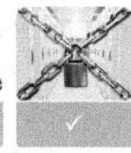    

Enforcing least privilege and separation of duties can go a long way towards limiting or even preventing the damage than could be inflicted by an insider threat. Controlling access, whether physical or technical, is a critical element in insider threat risk mitigation.

These least privilege and separation of duties catch phrases are often thrown about as solutions to the insider threat problem, but to many organizations the actual implementation is obscure at best. So let's take a look at what these mean and some of the possible implementations.

Least privilege

Least privilege is not a new concept. The original concept is attributed to Jerome Saltzer, who stated in the mid-1970s that "Every program and every privileged user of the system should operate using the least amount of privilege necessary to complete the job. It also reduces the number of potential interactions among privileged programs to the minimum for correct operation, so that unintentional, unwanted, or improper uses of privilege are less likely to occur. Thus, if a question arises related to misuse of a privilege, the number of programs that must be audited is minimized."[126] Applied to individuals, least privilege (also less commonly known as least authority) simply translates to granting the lowest level of access or rights that an individual can have and still perform their job. Or in other words, deny by default, allow by exception. By allowing only essential accesses and capabilities, the potential 'attack surface' is reduced.

But what exactly is a privilege? A privilege or set of privileges is the grouping of settings that define the permissions assigned to a user to execute certain tasks on the information system or network. All users require some level of privileges, such as those that allow individuals to create, modify, or delete files or folders. Others require the ability to make system-wide changes, like creating, modifying or deleting user accounts, altering security settings, or installing applications.

However, attempts to rein in privilege levels tend to be met with reluctance. Restricting privileges implies a certain lack of trust. Most users, whether thinking in terms of information system access or other physical forms of access, instinctively want the highest level of privilege possible. Senior leadership and managers in particular often expect enhanced control over their information systems, and may be dismissive of any limitation to their privileges. The tendency to give too many users administrative rights is a significant factor that increases the risks from insider threat.

Least privilege becomes more complex when thinking in terms of information systems and networking technology.

When considering least privilege for systems and networks, consider that the system/network is composed of a number of objects, each with its own level of protection requirements. Least privilege requires that the system have some way of knowing which individuals are authorized to have which access, and that the system has a reliable way to identify the user and the user's assigned accesses.

Devising a privilege access schema can be complex. Unix/Linux operating systems (OS) have long promoted least privilege. Microsoft only began making least privilege a feature with the release of the Windows XP and Windows 2000 OS. It became a key theme in Windows Vista OS when User Account Control (UAC) was introduced. In UAC, every type of account – including the built-in administrator accounts – has only limited user privileges by default. This was made possible by a new process of embedding access tokens within the OS for privileged account users. Each access token contains the user privileges and is attached to a user logon session. When a privileged user would log on to Windows Vista, two tokens were created: a full token and a filtered token. The filtered token functioned as the default token during the session and contained only the limited use privileges. The full token contained the user's enhanced privileges. Vista would attach the full token to the filtered token only when a user needed to perform an administrative task or initiate an application requiring privileged access.

With every Windows OS release, Microsoft continued to add new features. In Windows Server 2008, 2008 R2, 2012 R2 and Windows Server 2012, Active Directory (AD) has been designed to facilitate the delegation of rights and the principle of least privilege by assigning rights and permissions to specific user groups. General users are only allowed a limited set of privileges. A privileged user (PU) can be assigned to a specific built-in group in AD, which allows them only those granular rights and permissions essential for the performance of a specific function. These include Enterprise Admin (EA), Domain Admin (DA), and Administrators, and they are considered the highest privilege groups in AD.

An individual assigned to the EA group is placed in the forest* root domain and is, by default, a member of the Administrators group in all domains in the forest. EAs have rights and privileges that allow them to make changes that can affect the entire forest. EAs are followed by Domain Admins or DAs, who are members of that specific domain's Administrator group. Within their domain*, a DA is all-powerful and should only be assigned when high levels of privilege on *every* computer in the domain is required. The built-in local Administrator (BA) group has many of the privileges in the directory and on the domain controllers. Each of these groups has a default configuration, but there is an inherent weakness in that any member of any of these groups has the ability to manipulate AD in order to assign membership in any of the other groups. An assignment, therefore, to any of these groups should be well considered and any the actions of any individual assigned to these groups should be regularly

---

* The term 'forest' is used to apply to a part of a logical structure in the Microsoft AD. AD allows system administrators to organize network objects, e.g., users, devices, and computers, into a hierarchy of 'containers'. The forest is the top level container, and within the forest there are domains, and within the domains there are organizational units.
* A domain is a partition or container within the AD forest. Domains are generally used to logically organize objects and to enforce delegation of control at the appropriate administrative level. Organizational Units (OUs) are used within a domain to group objects, such as accounts, to further support delegation of authority. An OU can only contain objects from one domain.

audited. Below the domain level, there are organizational units, and privileges can be established for individual or for multiple organizational units.

The purpose of the above discussion of Windows AD is to illustrate that network and system privileges can be assigned at a level appropriate to the level of administrative requirements – and no higher. The actual process within Windows to assign these privileges is beyond the scope of this book, but there are a large number of Windows configuration guides that can assist in identifying and establishing privileges at the appropriate level. Microsoft's own website provides a wealth of information on using AD to enforce least privilege at *https://msdn.microsoft.com/en-us/library/bb742424.aspx?f=255&MSPPError=-2147217396*.

In addition to Windows, there are other operating systems that have different methods of applying the concepts of least privilege. These include UNIX and Linux, as well as the Apple operating systems. On Linux and UNIX platforms, system accounts, such as root or service accounts (e.g. Oracle), are needed for installation, configuration, system or network administration, and management tasks. There are a number of third-party applications that can assist system engineers in executing these tasks.

Least privilege can also apply to software code and applications. Just like a user, a piece of code should have only the privileges it needs to do the job. For example, many software developers still develop code that requires administrator privileges to work properly – even when that level of privilege is not absolutely essential.

When discussing these terms, one tends to think of them only in connection with information systems. However, these principles can apply equally to the physical environment. In the physical world, least privilege might mean limiting access to certain areas or at certain times of day.

Separation of Duties

Least privilege and separation of duties are linked. While each can be implemented without the other, employing complementary processes provides much greater security than just one. According to the *Common Sense Guide to Mitigating Insider Threats*, separation of duties is a classic security method that involves distributing functions among a number of individuals in order to restrict one individual from having unfettered access and the ability to unilaterally execute an insider attack.[127]

The two organizational areas at great risk from insider threat are information technology and financial asset management. Separation of duties, sometimes called segregation of duties, can assist in minimizing risk to these elements by implementing non-technical controls, such as policy and procedures, and/or technical controls. An example of a procedural control is requiring two individuals to be present when executing a transfer of sensitive or classified data, or executing peer reviews of software code.

In addition to defining roles and responsibilities, separation of duties may also include the separation of 'incompatible functions'. The US Institute of Internal Auditors (IIA) identifies custody of assets, authorizations and approvals, and recording and reporting as three key categories of incompatible duties. According to the IAA, work responsibilities should prevent any one person from having both access to and responsibility for accounting for financial and physical assets."[128] Fraud is one of the most common insider threat activities, and separation of duties is one of the most effective preventative measures. For example, financial institutions can implement a set of strong internal controls to ensure that no single individual has too much control over cash flow, financial data, inventory, or any other critical business asset.

A prerequisite for implementing separation of duties is establishing clear roles and associated responsibilities for individuals within the organization and using this to create appropriate segregation. Separation of duties may be simpler to accomplish in larger organizations with larger budgets and a larger staffing bench. This may be a challenge for smaller organizations with insufficient staff or with a tight budget. In this case, the only solution may be to implement processes that allow for checks and balances. For example, an organization may only have one system administrator, who may need to have full access to the system in order to perform the necessary functions; however, a second individual may be assigned to periodically review audit files to see if there has been any unauthorized activity.

The Quick Wins

- Create an information flow diagram for each function within the organization.
- Include separation of duties and least privilege early in the design of business processes and system configurations.
- Identify roles within the organizations and assign responsibilities based on the roles.

- Don't allow convenience or political expediency to trump security when assigning privileges.

Standards Mapping

STANDARD	CONTROL	SUBJECT
NIST 800-53, Security Controls for Federal Information Systems and Organizations	AC-5	Separation of Duties
	AC-6	Least Privilege
	PS-2	Position Risk Designation
ISO/IEC 27001:2013, Information technology– Security techniques– Information security management systems – Requirements	A10.1.3	Segregation of Duties
ISO/IEC 27002:2013, Information technology – Security techniques – Code of practice for information security management	10.1.3	Segregation of Duties
	11.2.2	Privilege Management

Recommendations for Additional Reading

Smith, Russell. *Least Privilege Security for Windows 7, Vista and XP. July 2010.* Packt Publishing Ltd., Birmingham, UK.

Desmond, Brian. *Active Directory: Designing, Deploying, and Running Active Directory, 5th Edition.* 2013. O'Reilly Media, Inc., Sebastapol, CA.

Anderson, Brian and Mulch, John. *Preventing Good People from Doing Bad Things: Implementing Least Privilege*. 12 October 2011. Apress Publishing.

13. Monitor and Audit Activities of General and Privileged Users

 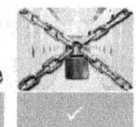    

With all of the recent newsworthy insider events, compliance and auditing programs are getting a lot of attention as a means of detecting and deterring insider threat activity. There are two primary types of audit: The first is a general audit or inspection focused on organizational processes. Standards, laws, and benchmarks are the primary sources for a baseline against which to conduct the audit.

The second is the technical audit of information systems, which involves the regular collection and review of the system-tracked system user activities. In this best practice, the focus is on the second form of audit and on the general and privileged users of information systems.

Auditing general and privileged user activities may be one of the primary means of deterrence, but can also serve as a source of after-the-fact forensic evidence. Despite this fact, a large number of organizations either do not audit, or they audit but have not implemented a systematic and regular review process.

So, what's the issue? Auditing and the associated reviews are often viewed as an administrative burden that is an add-on to the critical business processes. The benefit of integrating audit into core business processes is unrecognized. All organizations incur incremental costs to implement effective auditing, yet these resource and manpower costs are proportionally higher for smaller organizations.

Additionally, while the actual collection audit events are easy – the system does it for you – the settings for the items to be collected and the review of the audit logs is a time-consuming and often complicated effort. The possible settings, especially in a Windows Operating System (OS) or a Linux environment, are numerous, and determining what the most essential audit items are is not simple. Some organizations think authentication is critical; others focus on resource access; and yet others think that user account management is the most important control point.

Windows OS provides a number of integrated tools that support the auditing process. One of the most useful is the User Account Management Audit Policy, which allows audit for various user events to include: logon; logoff; object being changed, created, deleted, renamed or disabled; password changes; permission assignment changes; and a number of other actions. In Windows Server 2008 R2, for example, these settings can be accessed by going to Computer Configuration | Advanced Audit Policy Configuration | Account Management | User Account Management. Once the settings are determined, the audit settings can be managed centrally on the network with Group Policy and configured for event forwarding.

In Red Hat Linux, the Audit system provides a means to track and log security-relevant activities based on pre-configured rules. The Audit package is installed by default on Red Hat Enterprise Linux 6. Like the Windows OS, the Linux Audit system does not prevent security violations, but it can be used to discover security trespasses on the system.

Although there are auditing tools integrated into almost all operating systems, their use is often complicated and the audit logs themselves are difficult to acquire and review. Consequently, organizations may need additional tools in order to render the auditing process more manageable and useful.

CMU SEI's insider threat research revealed that a large majority of those insiders who committed IT sabotage or theft of organizational sensitive and classified information held privileged user positions. By the very definition of a privileged user, individuals in these positions have greater access to information systems and information, security mechanisms, networks, or applications.

According to CMU SEI, privileged users pose a special risk because they:

- have the technical ability and access authorizations to execute actions that exceed those of general users;
- can often hide their activities by using another user's login and credentials, by altering system logs, and/or by modifying or even deleting their audit trails.

Depending on the quality of audit, opportunity for the insider to capitalize on opportunities may be kept sufficiently low that no attack can be executed. CMU SEI research indicated that the "tipping point for an attack is an audit quality of between 68% and 69%."[129] Auditing is very useful in establishing normal computer use profiles for privileged users, as well as for general users, and can do much to enable the detection of abnormal patterns of activity.

While the collection of audit trails and logs is an excellent practice, it accomplishes little if adequate tools are not available to locate anomalies and misuse patterns that are displayed as raw data.

The Quick Wins

- Have all privileged users read and sign a Privileged User Agreement (PUA) or Rules of Behavior that clearly outlines their roles and responsibilities and which ensures actions can be taken if they violate the organization's trust. Maintain these agreements on file permanently, even after the departure of the individual.

- Require all privileged users to have both a privileged and general user account. Mandate that the privileged use account is only used when performing functions with enhanced privileged.

- Implement the concept of least privilege and limit all privileged users' access to only the functions essential to performing their assigned tasks.

- Conduct periodic audit reviews to detect any possible violation of privileged use.

Standards Mapping

STANDARD	CONTROL	SUBJECT
NIST 800-53, Security Controls for Federal Information Systems and	AU-2(4)	Audit Events: Privileged Functions

STANDARD	CONTROL	SUBJECT
Organizations		
	AU-9(4)	Protection of Audit Information: Access by Subset of Privileged Users
	IA-2(3)	Identification and Authentication (Organizational Users): Local Access to Privileged Accounts
	IA-2(8)	Identification and Authentication (Organizational Users): Network Access to Privileged Accounts
	SI-4(6)	Information System Monitoring: Restrict Non-Privileged Users
	SI-4(20)	Information System Monitoring: Privileged User
ISO/IEC 27001:2013, Information technology – Security techniques – Information security management systems – Requirements	A.11.2.2	Privilege Management
	A.11.2.4	Review of user access rights
ISO/IEC 27002:2013, Information technology – Security techniques – Code of practice for information security management	9.2	User access management
	9.2.3	Management of privileged access rights
	9.2.5	Review of user access rights

Recommendations for Additional Reading
Information Systems Audit and Control Association (ISACA). Information Systems Auditing: Tools and Technologies. Available at *www.isaca.org/Knowledge-Center/Research/ ResearchDeliverables/Pages/information-systems-auditing- tools-and-techniques.aspx* (requires membership)

14. Disable Access Immediately Upon Termination or Transfer

According to the US Bureau of Labor Statistics, the average number of years that employees remain with a private sector employer is 4.6 years as of January 2014. 21% of employees have one year of less tenure with an employer. Public sector employees tended to remain with their employer for an average of 7.8 years. Continued research indicates that these numbers will change as an increasing number of younger workers enter the work force, since they have proven to be more likely than older workers to be short-tenured.[130]

So, although an employer is normally not thinking about the possibility of termination or transfer when engaging a new employee, it is likely an inevitably that this situation will be faced at some time. So, here are some of the ways organizations can prepare for the inevitably of an employee's departure and ensure an efficient and secure termination or transfer:

- Develop policies and procedures that address all aspects of the termination process.

- Use a termination checklist to track all of the steps that are required for an effective and secure termination or transfer.

- Ensure the signed and completed termination checklist is returned to HR before the employee is allowed to leave the organization.

- Notify all entities in the organization of the employee's separation to prevent unauthorized access or the unintentional disclosure of information by former co-workers, with a simple message such as "John Doe has departed the company. Please do not disclose confidential information."

While all of the above actions are important, a comprehensive written checklist provides the greatest assurance that no items are left unaddressed. Below are a number of items that should be included on a checklist and which individuals/entities should be responsible. This list is not intended to be comprehensive; each organization should tailor its termination or transfer checklist to its own unique requirements.

Table 3: Employee Departure/Termination Checklist

Individual/Entity	Actions
Supervisor/Manager	Schedule and conduct exit interview
	Provide final performance appraisal
	Ensure final timesheet is completed
Finance	Ensure credit cards and purchase authorizations are retrieved
	Close all employee accounts
IT Security/System	Disable, not delete, all accounts

Individual/Entity	Actions
Administration	(retain for at least one year for investigative purposes)
	For privileged users, change any shared passwords for service accounts, network devices, etc.
	Collect any remote access tokens and disable any remote accounts and access privileges
	Update access lists to sensitive areas (e.g., server rooms, data centers, etc.)
	Remove employee from all automatic distribution lists and alerts
Facilities Security	Collect any badges, keys, access cards, parking passes, etc.
	Execute security debriefing
	Remove employee from all access lists
Records Department	Ensure employee returns company owned or controlled documents
IT Department	Ensure employee returns all equipment, e.g., software, laptop, tablet, mobile phone, etc.
	Verify returned equipment against inventory
	Ensure data files are retained on file, to include employee emails
HR Department	Complete separation paperwork
	Ensure employee is reminded of the stipulations in the NDA
	Notify all organizational entities of the separation

Anecdotal evidence indicates that not all physical or digital access authorizations are disabled or terminated when an employee separates from an organization, either by termination, cause-based transfer or restructuring of their duties. One of the most important actions is to disable – *not delete* – the individual's access immediately upon notification of termination or transfer for cause. Research by CMU SEI and other organizations indicates that many individuals engage in revenge-motivated insider threat activities after notice has been given, but before the employee actually departs the organization.

Why not delete access or accounts? Well, cases such as Snowden, indicate that access to the account activity and audit files can be essential even after an employee departs – especially in those cases that require additional investigation and forensic analysis. Recent events have indicated that organizations should consider retaining all disabled accounts and accesses on file for at least one year after the departure of the employee.

As a last recommendation, organizations should establish a process for reviewing a terminated/transferred employee's online actions for a period of 30 days prior to termination and continuing for at least 30 days after departure. What should be the focus of this review? Ensuring the employee has not emailed or executed an unauthorized download of any sensitive or prohibited organizational information.

As the discussion of the Cloud and insider threat indicated, this is a new and highly susceptible area for insider threat. Consequently, the organization must carefully audit or even block unauthorized transactions to ensure that an employee does not move organizational information to the Cloud.

The Quick Wins

- Implement an enterprise-wide checklist and enforce its use.

- Ensure all employee accesses are tracked.

- Disable access and archive all accounts associated with a terminated/transferred employee.

- Monitor, or even block, all access to non-corporate Cloud storage providers.

- Establish an inventory system to track all asset issued to an employee, and conduct regular inventories.

Standards Mapping

STANDARD	CONTROL	SUBJECT
NIST 800-53, Security Controls for Federal Information Systems and Organizations	PS-4	Personnel Termination
	PS-5	Personnel Transfer
ISO/IEC 27001:2013, Information technology – Security techniques – Information security management systems – Requirements	A.7.3.1	Termination or change of employment responsibilities
	A.8.1.4	Return of assets
ISO/IEC 27002:2013, Information technology – Security techniques – Code of practice for information security management	8.3.1	Termination responsibilities
	8.3.2	Return of assets
	8.3.3	Removal of access rights

Recommendations for Additional Reading
Australian Government personnel security protocol. April 2015. Available at *www.protectivesecurity.gov.au/ personnelsecurity/Pages/Australian-Government-personnel-security-management-protocol.aspx*

15. Address the Challenges of the External or Temporary 'Insider'

 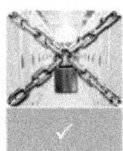   

Frequently persons may be considered 'insiders for a limited period of time, including consultants, support contractors, partners, service providers, and/or temporary employees.* These individuals may require authorized access to organizational facilities, internal infrastructure, information technology and sensitive data. For example, if an organization contracts an outside entity to provide Cloud services, it may have to provide access to the areas where critical data is stored. A facilities maintenance contract would allow authorized outsiders access to the physical infrastructure. An IT service contract would authorize a

---

* For the purposes of this discussion, a contractor is an external employee hired under a contractual arrangement between the organization and the contract entity; a temporary employee is any individual hired for a short period of time; a consultant is someone who performs specific services for the organization; a partner is another organization with which a form of alliance exists; and a service provider is any organization that may provide specified services, such as legal, storage, security, etc.

non-organic organization access to the IT infrastructure. As a result, "The boundary of the organization's enterprise needs to be drawn broadly enough to include as Insiders all people who have a privileged understanding of and access to the organization, its information, and information systems."[131]

It is not uncommon for the external/temporary insider to have access to an organization's critical physical and digital assets. Contracts or agreements that require or include authorized access to organizational assets should also contain a requirement for compliance with the security policies and procedures. Special care is needed with such individuals to ensure that physical and digital access is appropriately restricted and removed when their activities are completed.

In the report Spotlight On: Insider Threat from Trusted Business Partners, CMU SEI provided a set of recommendations specifically for organizations concerned about malicious acts from trusted partners. Many of these may sound much like the best practices recommended for insiders within the organization; others are specifically focused on the requirements of the trusted partner relationship. So, here is a summary of the recommendations:[132]

- Understand the culture and policies of the trusted partner.

- Ensure there are mechanisms in place to monitor the access to critical organizational information.

- Manage any access provided by the primary trusted partner to sub-partners.

- Ensure all accesses for primary trusted partners and sub-partners are removed immediately upon termination of the agreement or when personnel are transferred.

- Implement clear, precise contractual and/or service level agreements that include all security requirements the trusted partner is required to meet, and the ramifications if these requirements are not met.

One note: Costs imposed on consultants or contractors as part of this requirement may become an increased contract cost.

The Quick Wins

- Ensure security requirements for primary and secondary trusted partners are included in all contracts and service level agreements.

- Maintain a strict policy of least privilege for all trusted partners and monitor all accesses.

Standards Mapping

STANDARD	CONTROL	SUBJECT
NIST 800-53, Security Controls for Federal Information Systems and Organizations	AC-5	Least Privilege
	PS-7	Third Party Personnel Security
ISO/IEC 27001:2013, Information technology – Security techniques – Information security management systems – Requirements	A.6.2.1	Identification of risks related to external parties

STANDARD	CONTROL	SUBJECT
	A.6.2.3	Addressing security in third party agreements
ISO/IEC 27002:2013, Information technology – Security techniques – Code of practice for information security management	15.1	Information security in supplier relationships
	15.1.2	Addressing security in supplier agreements
	15.2.1	Monitoring and review of supplier services
	A.8.1.4	Return of assets

Recommendations for Additional Reading

Cole, Dr. Eric and Ring, Sandra. *Insider Threat: Protecting the Enterprise from Sabotage, Spying and Theft*. 15 March 2006. Syngress Publishing.

Kendrick, Rupert. *Outsourcing IT – A governance guide*. 26 November 2009. IT Governance Publishing.

Desai, Jimmy. *Service Level Agreements: A legal and practical guide*. 21 October 2010. IT Governance Publishing.

Prevention and Deterrence

16. Layer Defenses to Provide Defense-in-Depth

Any single tool or process may have defects that reduce or even disable its effectiveness. A layered defense combines multiple heterogeneous tools and processes, employed such that one tool or process protects against the weaknesses of the other(s). Layered defenses can be applied in both the digital and analogue environments. Lately, it seems as if everyone is talking about layered security and defense-in-depth – but how many know what this really means? The concept of multiple layers of defensive measures originated in a military context, where a strategy involved the implementation of a comprehensive set of security controls.

First of all, it is important, however, to understand the small distinction between a layered defense and a defense-in-depth. A layered defense implies a singular focus designed "to protect systems that behave within certain common parameters or activity from threats those activities may attract."[133] Defense-in-depth implies a set of mutually-supportive defensive measures – consisting of personnel, processes, and technologies – designed to absorb and progressively weaken or deter the attacker.

Regardless of the definition, the basic idea is clear – any single defense may be flawed, and in both the physical and digital environments, no defense is completely impenetrable. Consequently, a layered defense consisting of several mutually supportive technologies and processes provides the most effective method for hindering the progress of a threat, by either slowing it or frustrating it until the threat either ceases its activities or is detected.

The same concept of providing a series of defensive layers applies equally to the physical and the digital environments, with each layer supporting the other to deter an unwanted intrusion or other insider threat activity. The controls applied seek the same results – to deter or delay, detect, and recover.

Physical Defenses

Physical security has been present in many forms, for as long as mankind has existed. Physical insider threats are largely driven by the same motives as digital insider threats: financial greed, revenge, advancement of a personal agenda, and others. The primary objective of physical defense, therefore, is to deter an individual from gaining unauthorized access to a protected physical location. Physical defense and deterrence lies primary in the application of barriers, whether physical or psychological. Physical barriers take the form a fences, walls, gates, locks, or even natural barriers, such as plants. Psychological barriers often occur within personnel access control areas, where visitors are required to register prior to being allowed access and where employees must badge in or otherwise verify their identity for access. *Figure 30* illustrates a layered physical security defense.

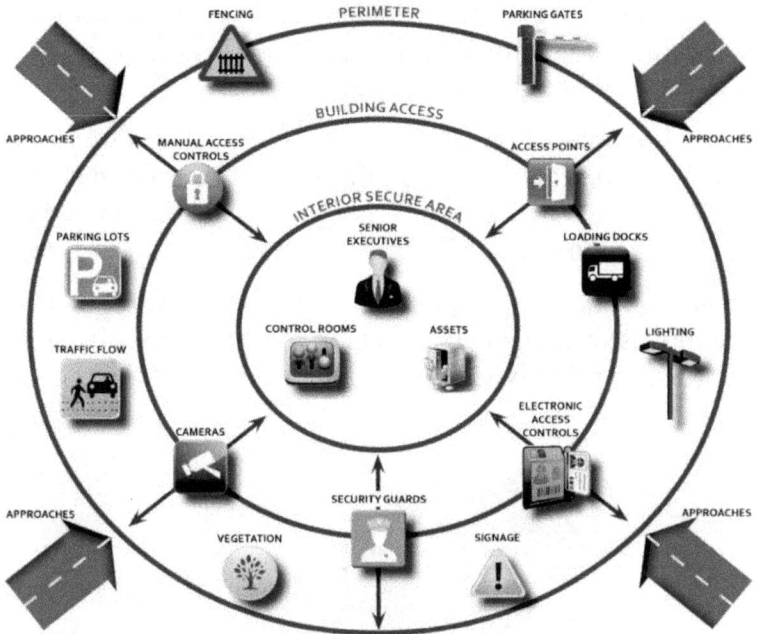

Source: Corporate Risk Solutions, www.corprisk.net/services/physical-security/service-details

Figure 30: Layered physical defenses

Effective physical defenses also support the digital defensive mechanisms by restraining access to the network workstations and servers.

Digital Defenses

Recent events have led to extensive focus on the dangers of insider threat to information and information systems. Consequently, much more time has been spent in detailing how to employ layered digital defenses against the insider threat. In the technical environment, like the physical, the "concurrent employment of protection tools of different origins and the same fundamental purpose provides variability in the technical approach to protection. This increases the likelihood of success".[134]

Thus a combination of policies, physical controls, and technical controls, such as firewalls, intrusion detection systems, malware scanners, integrity auditing procedures and encryption tools, can serve to protect digital resources.

Figure 31 illustrates a physical and digital layered defense that moves from data and assets to physical controls, policy controls, and finally to technical controls.

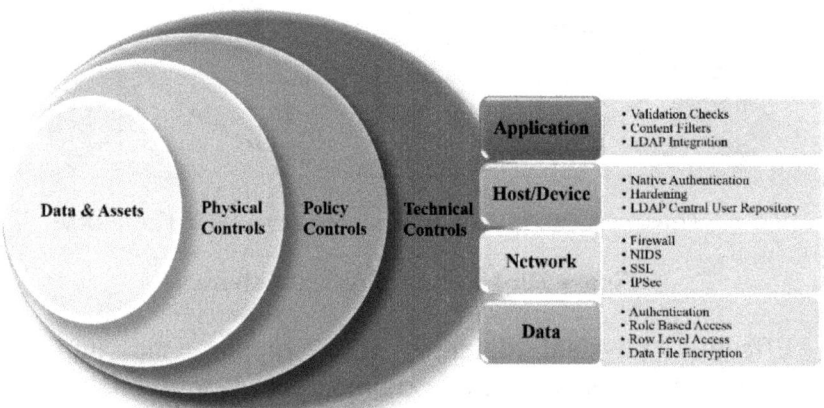

Figure 31: Digital defense-in-depth

Very large amounts of manpower and resources have been directed towards the creation of perimeter defenses, such as firewalls and intrusion detection systems (IDS). It is true that firewalls and IDS provide a very useful defense against a malicious outsider – however, IDS are typically not configured to focus internally and monitor the activities of insiders. By positioning IDS at multiple levels *within* the information system network, more attention can be directed towards detecting anomalous insider activity – and to spotting not only activity associated with attempts to enter the system, but also egress from the system.

CMU SEI has proposed an Insider Threat Security Reference Architecture (ITSRA) designed to provide a layered, enterprise-level solution to the insider threat problem. The ITSRA is comprised of four layers: business, information, data and application. In order for the ITSRA to be successful, each of these layers must function in close relationships to the others. The CMU SEI ITSRA is consistent with the layers illustrated in *Figure 31* above, but goes further to look at how existing best practices and security architectures can be applied. *Figure 32* provides an adaptation of a sample subset of security controls aligned to the ITSRA layers.

	Access	Acceptable Use	Continuous Monitoring
Business	• Legal counsel • Organization Policy • Physical security • Need to know	• Legal counsel • Organization Policy • Acceptable use policy	• Legal counsel • Organization Policy • Continuous assessment • Change management
Information	• Account Management • Host-based IDS • Authentication	• Firewalls • Proxy • IDS/IPS • File level access restrictions • Least privilege	• Audit log correlation • Automated alerts • Incident response
Data	• Account management • Role based access	• Data classification • Data labeling • Least privilege	• Data leakage protection • Intrusion detection
Application	• Account management • Separation of duties • Software library management	• Code review • Quality assurance	• Software development peer reviews • Configuration and change management

Figure 32: Adaptation of the ITSRA sample subset of controls per ITSRA layer

Since insider threats are likely to exploit weaknesses in more than one layer, vertical alignment of security countermeasures is critical to success in providing detection or deterrence. According to the ITSRA, "Any controls meant to enforce physical access to a closed area should also be extended into the logical realms of information, data, and application controls. Information controls may involve the existence of a dedicated account for [a] particular individual inside the closed area, along with multifactor authentication to confirm that individual's identity. Moving down to the data layer, file access controls for read-write privileges must be in place to restrict the individual's need-to-know access. For instance, an employee dedicated to biological research should not have any read access to internal salary records. Finally, if the closed area contains any sensitive applications, those applications must have appropriate safeguards in place to ensure authorized access. Using [an] investment trader as an example… if portions of the code should not have been accessible to him, a code management system such as CVS* should have been in place to restrict his access."[135]

The Quick Wins

- Establish procedures for vertically aligning insider threat countermeasures across the corporate functions, information and data protection, and applications.

- Define requirements at the highest level in the organization and implement relevant security countermeasures through the ITSRA layers.

---

* CVS refers to the Concurrent Versions System, which manages the activities of multiple software developers. It is an opensource capability and can be acquired at *http://ftp.gnu.org/non-gnu/cvs/*.

- Deploy firewalls and intrusion detection systems (IDS) internally to enforce compartmentalization of information systems and information assets.

Standards Mapping

STANDARD	CONTROL	SUBJECT
NIST 800-53, Security Controls for Federal Information Systems and Organizations	AT-3(4)	Security Training | Suspicious Communications and Anomalous System Behavior
	PL-8	Information Security Architecture
	PL-8(1)	Information Security Architecture: Defense in Depth
	SC-32	Information System Partitioning
ISO/IEC 27001:2013, Information technology – Security techniques– Information security management systems – Requirements	6.1	Planning: Actions to address risks and opportunities
	8.3	Operation: Information security risk treatments
ISO/IEC 27002:2013, Information technology – Security techniques – Code of practice for information security management	9.2	System and application access
	11	Operations security
	14	System acquisition, development and maintenance

Recommendations for Additional Reading
Small, Prescott E. *Defense in Depth – An Impractical Strategy for a Cyber World.* November 2011. CreateSpace Independent Publishing Platform.
Woody, Aaron. *Enterprise Security: A Data-Centric Approach to Securing the Enterprise.* February 2013. Packt Publishing.

17. Conduct Regular Evaluations of Security Controls

Thorough and regular evaluations of the effectiveness of security controls is a vital element in determining whether or not an organization is compliant with its own policies, processes, and standards. Almost every insider threat event can be tracked back to a weakness in the people, processes or technologies (or all three!). Assessments generally use one or more of the following methods: testing, examination (document review and observation), and interviews.

Evaluating an organization's security control compliance begins with a knowledge of the organization's policies, security governance structure, and security processes and procedures. Start with the organization's own policies, then design the compliance evaluations against existing laws, standards, and benchmarks; some of the most prevalent include:

- NIST 800 and ISO/IEC 2700 series standards;

- Laws such as the U.S. Gramm-Leach-Bliley Act (GLBA), Sarbanes-Oxley Act (SOX), UK Data Protection Act, the European Union Network and Information Security;

- Center for Internet Security (CIS) Benchmarks.

There are also numerous assessment methodologies that can support the process:

- Security design reviews – designed to assess the deployment of the technologies for compliance and effectiveness using network architecture and engineering tests.

- Security process reviews – designed to identify flaws in the execution of policies and procedures.

- Social engineering tests – testing employees for unintentional vulnerabilities, specifically to determine if security awareness training is effective.

- Technical assessments – using methodologies, such as penetration testing and vulnerability scans, to evaluate the effectiveness of security tools and technologies.

Compliance evaluation and testing is not necessarily just a formal discipline – it is an art form. It requires a certain mindset to figure out new weaknesses and the associated exploit techniques – not unlike that of a hacker! Any controls evaluation or inspection team must have a base knowledge of testing tools and techniques to complement their understanding of compliance requirements.

Successful evaluations also require a methodological approach. There are several common methods available, including:

- The **Open Source Security Testing Methodology Manual (OSSTMM)**. OSSTMM is an openly-available manual for conducting security testing in a comprehensive and repeatable manner. The methodology has six interconnected testing modules for information security, process security, Internet technologies security, communications security, wireless security, and physical security. OSSTMM Version 3 is available free from the ISECOM at: *www.isecom.org/mirror/OSSTMM.3.pdf*

- The **Information Systems Security Assessment Framework (ISSAF)** created by the Open Information Systems Security Group (OISSG), is one of the most comprehensive free assessment methodologies. It weighs in at over 1200 pages with a staggering level of detail. It's an older standard, dated 2006, but the evaluation processes are still relevant and it is available for free. Download at *http://wiki.dksh.com.br/Downloads/ security/issaf0.2.1b.pdf*.

- **US National Institute of Standards and Technology (NIST) Special Publication (SP) 800-115,** *Technical Guide to Information Security Testing*. SPs are considered standards, and NIST SP 800-115 provides guidance for reviewing security against US laws and security standards. The SP includes a number of templates, techniques and tools for numerous scenarios and system types. While not as detailed as the two standards above, it does offer repeatable processes for conducting security testing. The document is available for free at *http://csrc.nist.gov/publications/nistpubs/800-115/SP800-115.pdf*.

- **Open Web Application Security Project (OWASP) Testing Guide.** Although the OWASP Testing Guide was designed primarily to assist web developers and security personnel to design and implement more secure web applications, it provides tools, guides and testing methodologies that have a broader applicability. The OWASP Testing Guide can be downloaded from *www.owasp.org/images/5/52/OWASP_Testing_Guide_v4. pdf.*

Technical Testing

Regardless of the methodology chosen, it must be repeatable. This provides consistency and structure to the security assessment process, and is particularly critical when executing technical assessments, where no single technique can provide a fully inclusive picture of a system or a network. While technical testing goes beyond other methods to provide an accurate picture of the organization's system security posture, it is potentially more intrusive and could impact systems or networks in the target assessment environment. A repeatable process allows organizations to better determine the acceptable level of intrusiveness and the potential for unexpected system behavior.

External vs Internal Testing

Testing can be executed from the viewpoint of an external attacker or an insider – or both. External testing is generally conducted from outside the organization's perimeter. This allows for the testers to view the organization's security configurations as they appear to an outsider, and the objective is to identify weaknesses that could potentially be exploited by an external invader. External testing generally begins with reconnaissance of any publicly available information that may help the assessor to identify weaknesses, such as Internet

Protocol (IP) addresses, operating systems, system names, etc. Next, the tester will enumerate the network, using network discovery and scanning tools and techniques to identify whether there are external hosts and perimeter defenses in place, as well to see if any exploitable protocols or services are being used. Since the goal of this external testing is to emulate a hacker, understanding how hackers work and the tools they use is crucial to developing the appropriate perspective. AltiusIT developed a list of the top ten tools that is inclusive of just about anything an external tester might need in their toolbox:[136]

1. *Reconnaissance.* Hackers use tools to get basic information on your systems. For example, tools like Netcraft and PCHels can report on domain, IP number, and operating system.

2. *Network exploration.* The more information the hacker knows about the system, the more ways he can find vulnerabilities. Tools such as NMap identify host systems and services.

3. *Probe tools.* Some tools were initially designed to be used by system administrators to enhance their security. Now, these same tools are used by hackers to know where to start an attack. Tools like LANguard Network Security Scanner identify system vulnerabilities.

4. *Scanners.* Internally, sniffer tools analyze network performance and applications. Hacker reconnaissance tools such as AET Network Scanner 10, FPort 1.33, and Super Scan 3 scan devices to determine ports that are open and can be exploited.

5. *Password cracker.* Password tools are used by security administrators to find weak passwords. These tools may also be used by hackers. Password crackers include LC5,

John The Ripper, iOpus Password Recovery XP, and LastBit.

6. ***Remote administration tools.*** Tools such as AntiLamer and NetSlayer are used by hackers to take partial or complete control of the victim's computer.

7. ***Backdoor.*** Backdoor tools and Trojan Horses exploit vulnerabilities and open systems to a hacker. KrAIMer and Troj/Zinx-A can be used by hackers to gain access to your systems.

8. ***Denial-of-service (DoS).*** Denial-of-service attacks overload a system or device so it can't respond or provide normal service. Hackers use tools such as Coldlife and Flooder to overload a system (these are *not* recommended for normal technical testing).

9. ***Recover deleted files.*** Once hackers are inside the perimeter, they can use tools like Deleted File Analysis Utility to scan hard drive partitions for deleted files that may still be recoverable.

10. ***Website tools.*** Hackers use tools such as AccessDiver and IntelliTamper to index website pages and directories. These tools can download the site to the hacker's local hard drive. Once on his system, the hacker can analyze the website to identify and exploit security vulnerabilities.

For the purpose of internal testing, the evaluators are generally granted a level of access to the system – either as a general user or as a privileged user. Sometimes both levels of access are used in order to develop a more comprehensive picture. Often, commercial vulnerability scanning tools are used during an internal test. These tools are generally benign and can scan the network and websites for thousands of pre-determined security risks, produce a prioritized list of those requiring mitigation, describe the weaknesses, and even provide advice on how to remediate them. Some can even automate the patching process (although this should be approached with caution – if at all possible, *never* patch on operational systems and do not choose the option 'Remediate all' when it is presented by the scanning tool). There are a large number of for-purchase scanning tools, but for cash-strapped organizations, there are also a number of highly successful free tools. The list below provides a sample of some of the more common openly accessible tools:

- **Open Vulnerability Assessment System (OpenVAS)** is a free network scanner available via a number of Linux packages or as a downloadable virtual appliance. Note – this scanner does not work on Windows systems.

- **Retina CS Community** offers vulnerability scanning and patching for Windows OS and common third-party applications, such as Adobe and Firefox. It scans the network for vulnerabilities, configuration issues, and missing patches.

- **Microsoft Baseline Security Analyzer (MBSA)** is able to execute local or remote scans on Windows OS desktops and servers, looking for missing service packs, security patches, and common misconfigurations.

- **Nexpose Community Edition** is designed to scan networks, operating systems, web applications, databases, and virtual environment. Although this tools is free, the free version has a 32 IP limit, which may make this tool less practical for larger networks.

- **SecureCheq** conducts local scans on Windows OS desktops and servers, looking for insecure settings as defined by CIS, ISO, or COBIT standards. It concentrates on common configuration errors related to

OS hardening, data protection, communication security, user account activity, and audit logging. The free version is only able to scan a little over 20 settings, about one quarter of those scanned by the for-purchase tool.

- **Qualsys FreeScan** provides up to 10 free scans of URLs and IPs on Internet-facing or local servers.

- **Arachni** is a free web application security scanner. It is a smart tool, which means that it trains itself by learning from the HTTP responses it receives during the assessment process.

- **W3af** is an open-source web application audit framework written in Python. This tool has both a graphical use interface and a command line interface and uses more than 130 plugins to identify web application vulnerabilities.

A word of warning: technical testing alone cannot provide a full evaluation of an organization's overall security posture. It generally has a much narrower scope and can only represent a moment in time, and while an organization may be reluctant to use a technique or tool that could have a potential for negative impact, a malicious outsider or insider threat does not have the same limitation. Consequently, combining testing and other more holistic assessment techniques can provide a more accurate view of the organization's real security status.

The Quick Wins

- Identify tools specific to the system and/or network environment.

- Determine an appropriate timeframe for scanning the system (e.g., daily, weekly, monthly) and execute regularly.

- Ensure results of scans are analyzed to identify weaknesses needing remediation.
- Review scan results for lessons learned to implement as part of a continuous improvement program.

Standards Mapping

STANDARD	CONTROL	SUBJECT
NIST 800-53, Security Controls for Federal Information Systems and Organizations	AT-3(4)	Security Training: Suspicious Communications and Anomalous System Behavior
	AU-6(5)	Audit Review, Analysis and Reporting | Central Review and Analysis
	CA-2	Security Assessments
	RA-5	Vulnerability Scanning
ISO/IEC 27001:2013, Information technology – Security techniques – Information security management systems – Requirements	A.12.6	Technical vulnerability management
	A.12.6.1	Control of technical vulnerabilities
ISO/IEC 27002:2013, Information technology – Security techniques – Code of practice for information security management	12.6	Technical vulnerability management
	12.6.1	Management of technical vulnerabilities
	18.2.3	Technical compliance review

Recommendations for Additional Reading
Wysopal, Chris; Nelson, Lucas; Dai Zovi, Dino; and Dustin, Elfriede. *The Art of Software Security Testing: Identifying Software Security Flaws.* November 2006. Addison-Wesley Professional Publishers.
Henry, Kevin M. *Penetration Testing – Protecting Networks and Systems.* 21 June 2012. IT Governance Publishing.
Course Technology. *Network Defense – Security and Vulnerability Assessment.* 19 April 2010. EC-Council Publisher.
Michajlowsky, Andriej; Gavrilenko, Konstantin; and Vladmirow, Andrew. *Assessing Information Security: Strategies, Tactics, Logic and Framework.* 29 January 2015. IT Governance Publishing.

18. Limit, Monitor and Control Remote Access and Mobile Device Use

The term 'remote access' can mean a number of things. It can be used by system administrators as a means to remotely connect to a corporate network, generally for the purposes of remote administration and most often when it is difficult or impractical to physically access the system or network. The other form of remote access is allowing users the ability to gain access to a system or network from an off-site location via a dedicated line or – more commonly – through a remote access server which is part of a virtual private network (VPN). For the purposes of this section, the focus is on the second form of remote access.

Increasing numbers of workers engage in either full or part-time teleworking and are using a number of remote access technologies, such as laptops, home workstations, tablets, and smartphones. Remote access to a corporate network via the Internet has added a completely new dimension to the challenge of keeping critical information and resources secure. The extent of remote access and the associated security requirements will vary from simple to very complex depending on the needs of the organization.

Add the use of mobile technologies to remote access and the problem is compounded. The use of mobile technologies is not new, but more employees are demanding the ability to use their own devices – commonly called Bring Your Own Device (BYOD) – in their corporate environments and certainly during telework or when on business travel. A newly-mobile workforce, together with blurred boundaries caused by mobile technologies and BYOD, has elevated the risk of a potential insider attack.

Between teleworkers and ever-more capable mobile devices, organizations are challenged to enable secure access for an increasing number of employees while simultaneously grappling with reduced resources and increased compliance mandates. Ensuring that no unauthorized users gain access to internal resources is only one aspect of the remote access security problem. The other side of the challenge is ensuring that insiders do not abuse remote access capability and/or the use of their own mobile devices to compromise the organization and its information. Let's take a look at the challenges of telework, aka telecommuting, first.

Remote Access, Telework and Insider Threat Challenges

Many organizations appreciate the cost savings inherent in allowing employees to telework, while employees benefit from the convenience of telecommuting. For those of us who live in areas where the average commute takes over one hour, the benefits are clear! In addition, employees may have a need to connect back to the corporate network from home when they are on the road, in the evenings, or on the weekends. The same remote access could be provided to a consultant or partner, who works from a home office, or to a 'road warrior' who spends a great deal of time working in airports, hotel rooms, or the local Starbucks.

All this results in a lot of remote access connections that could easily provide a potential insider threat with a rich source of corporate information. When an organization's systems are opened to external access, a number of security risks are introduced. The severity of these risks is often related to the system literacy of the individual accessing the system or the network. Also, considering how over-burdened the IT staff may already be, it becomes increasingly difficult to maintain and audit non-centralized information systems. So, while many organizations may face challenges from the unintentional user error, insiders can present a very different problem when operating in a remote environment. Insider threats have actually admitted "that it is easier to conduct malicious activities from home [or other locations] because it eliminates the concern that a co-worker could be physically observing the malicious acts."[137]

Since providing remote access capability is no longer an option for many organizations, both operational managers and IT staff should consider what can be done to make the process as secure as possible. There are a number of actions that can be taken to make remote connections more secure.

Telecommuting Policy

The first step is defining a telecommuting security policy. At minimum, a remote access security policy should consider:

- required equipment, operating system and business software;
- physical security guidelines to protect the equipment when off-site;
- measures that must be taken to protect the integrity and security of organizational information, such as backup, secure transmission, etc.;
- disaster recovery in the event of theft or destruction of the equipment or corruption of the data;
- maintenance requirements, such as update schedules for antivirus or system patching;
- individual accountability for the equipment and the information;
- personal use guidelines, if appropriate.

Each remote user should be required to read and understand the policy and sign a verification form that is retained on file for reference and accountability.

Determining Who Needs Remote Access

An organization may not be able to handpick those users who require remote access. The determination can also be based on a number of external factors, such as client demands, employee illness or injury, the requirement for employee travel, and other events. Still, an organization has some control over placement of employees in positions authorized for remote access. The primary factors to consider are the organization's and the employee's needs and the employee's qualifications when it comes to computer literacy and security awareness.

So, how can the need for remote access be determined? Generally, the job function, percentage of required travel, and the requirement for remote access to current corporate information will help define the requirement. Alternatively, the organization may have a general policy for authorizing extensive telecommuting as part of its own resource conservation needs.

Any employee allowed remote access should have the appropriate authorization for the level of access requested, and the need for access should be continually evaluated as job functions and requirements change. Finally, any individual authorized to have remote access should demonstrate a level of computer literacy that would enable the worker to perform simple maintenance activities, such as backup.

Conduct Remote Access Security Awareness Training

Just because an individual knows how to use the organization's IT equipment and software, this does not necessarily mean that they are aware of the remote access security and protection requirements. Remote access brings with it a number of additional requirements, such as ensuring the system (particularly a BYOD system) has firewall protection, sufficient antivirus protection, and the means to encrypt data, if required. Each remote access worker must be thoroughly trained in the security and protection requirements and have hands-on training in the correct operation of the technology and basic troubleshooting techniques.

Remote access workers should also have an enhanced awareness of general security procedures. For example, an individual who will not open an unfamiliar email attachment when at the work site may not be as vigilant on the personal computer they are using to connect remotely to corporate systems or networks. The same user may take for granted that the 'free' wireless access they get at the local Starbucks is as secure as the wireless access at their corporate work site.

At a minimum, remote access security training should include the following:

- information on risks to the organization's information assets and the assets of other entities that may be interconnected;
- details of potential risks when individuals are allowed use of BYOD;
- requirements for device security, such as antivirus, firewalls, etc.;
- protection of remote access authenticators, such as passwords, tokens, smart cards;
- ways to recognize social engineering attacks and appropriate actions;

- consequences for disabling, altering, or attempts to circumvent the security configurations;

- security incident reporting procedures;

- emphasis on protecting information assets from unauthorized access and use by others, including family members and friends;

- ensuring information assets and devices are left only in secure locations and not where they might be easily stolen or hacked;

- how to implement physical security controls when appropriate;

- statement on the risk of using public wireless hotspots;

- requirement to limit work when in the presence of visitors/strangers.

Selecting Appropriate Remote Access Technologies

There are a number of technologies that can potentially enhance remote access security. These include the use of one-time passwords, smart cards or tokens, or other alternatives to traditional login and passwords; the use of an email proxy that allows users to check email without requiring access to the corporate networks; and implementation of encrypted channels, such as encrypted virtual private networks (VPNs). VPNs can be designed to provide end-to-end security between remote workers and corporate networks. They employ the point-to-point tunneling protocol (PPP) to establish a secure connection, or tunnel, through the organization's firewall. A VPN can employ digital certificate technology to authenticate remote users.

The technologies allowing remote access must be accompanied by sufficient monitoring that allows tracking, auditing, and reporting of remote access activity. Monitoring is essential to identifying usage patterns and unusual network activity, as well as measuring the effectiveness of the remote access technologies. Identifying remote access technologies and implementing the selected technologies *prior* to authorizing any remote access is critical.

One final thought: As crucial as it is to manage remote access for an employee or partner, it is often even more important to ensure that remote access is disabled as part of any employee separation or termination process. With this in mind, the following actions should be part of the termination process:

- Disable any remote access accounts;
- Retrieve any remote access tokens or smart cards;
- Retrieve any corporate owned equipment and software.

Mobile Technologies

There is no way to stem the exploding use of mobile devices. Organizations should therefore consider a 'mobile first' mindset when planning their remote access policies and configurations. Risks are increasing as more and more mobile devices are used almost seamlessly between public and private networks.

If an organization elects to allow remote access, or telework, it should seriously consider providing teleworking employees with corporate-owned and configured equipment – but today, more and more individuals are choosing to use their own mobile devices to access their organization's systems or networks. These personally-owned devices may not be subject to many of the appropriate use policies that apply to on-site equipment, are not audited on a regular basis, and are generally not subject to control.

Before allowing the use of personally-owned mobile devices, the organization must consider the increased risk posed by a user connecting to the systems or network with their own devices. Risks can include unauthorized access to the organization's information assets, the commingling of personal and corporate information on personally-owned devices, and the challenges associated with litigation, e-discovery, forensic, and audit processes on non-corporate devices.

Smart devices can now place the functionality of a desktop computer into a hand-held device. Many of these devices have integrated cameras and recording capability. Photos of sensitive physical facility aspects or organizational information can be easily captured by a mobile device, then sent to a social media site, a personal computer, or even to the Cloud. As a result, each organization should carefully consider the risk of allowing employee-owned devices onto the physical site, much less allowing connection to corporate systems/networks.

Further, smart devices can use the cellular phone network to access the Internet or allow VPN access to the corporate network via a laptop or other device. These... are entry points into the corporate network that need to be monitored and controlled. If users can bridge their trusted, corporate connection with an untrusted, tethered connection, then they could completely bypass all enterprise network security by directing their illicit activity though the unmonitored connection.[138] As a result, organizations should treat any mobile device as a form of removable media and apply the same security requirements to them.

The Quick Wins

- Plan remote access security when working out the remote access solution.

- Create and configure remote access policies. Use remote access policies to define the requirements and conditions that users must match in order to obtain remote access.

- Create and configure remote access profiles. Identify those users that need remote access and configure only these individuals to have remote access.

- Configure remote access authentication and encryption.

- Monitor and control all remote access endpoints.

- Ensure all employees read and sign a remote access and/or mobile device Acceptable Use Policy.

- Disable all forms of remote access and retrieve any company equipment and software when an employee separates or is terminated.

Standards Mapping

STANDARD	CONTROL	SUBJECT
NIST 800-53, Security Controls for Federal Information Systems and Organizations	AC-17	Remote Access
	AT-3	Role-Based Security Training
	IA-2(11)	Identification and Authentication (Organizational Users)	Remote access – separate device
	SC-7(7)	Boundary Protection	Prevent Split Tunneling

STANDARD	CONTROL	SUBJECT
		for Remote Devices
ISO/IEC 27001:2013, Information technology – Security techniques – Information security management systems – Requirements	A.11.4.4	Remote Diagnostic and configuration port protection
ISO/IEC 27002:2013, Information technology – Security techniques – Code of practice for information security management	6.2	Mobile devices and teleworking
	6.2.1	Mobile device policy
	6.2.2	Teleworking

Recommendations for Additional Reading
Kasacavage, Victor. *Complete Book of Remote Access: Connectivity and Security*. 10 December 2002. Auerbach Publications.

19. Obtain Explicit Security Agreements for Cloud Services

As discussed earlier in the book, a large number of private and public organizations have been moving their information to the Cloud. According to the National

Institute of Standards and Technology (NIST), Cloud computing is "a model for enabling ubiquitous, convenient, on-demand network access to a shared pool of configurable computing resources (e.g. networks, servers, storage, applications, and services) that can be rapidly provisioned and released *with minimal management effort or service provider interaction* [italics added]."[139]

The benefit of Cloud computing – a shared environment with limited interaction – is also the very characteristic that causes security concerns. The Cloud service provider is generally external to the service customer's environment and direct control. Organizations must rely on the Cloud service provider's self-attestation that the security policies and procedures provide the organization with the required level of security.

Protecting the organization against insider threats who exploit weaknesses related to Cloud service characteristics is challenging, but can be addressed with a combination of diligence and planning when procuring, transitioning to, and using Cloud services. One way to protect the organization against the insider threat, as well as any other security-related threat, is to develop a strong set of ground rules and a plan for when things go awry, so that an expected level of service and security is maintained.

It is common for a contracting company to require a blueprint for the construction of a new building or for a customer to expect a warranty when buying a new car. A detailed service level agreement (SLA) or contract can serve as the blueprint and the warranty for Cloud services. The SLA/contract set expectations for both the Cloud service provider and the customer.

At a minimum, the SLA/contract should address the following:

- specific parameters and minimum levels required for each service element, as well as the repercussions for failure to meet the requirements;
- availability of services and data; for example, 99.9% during work days and 99% for nights/weekends;
- disaster recovery expectations;
- data encryption requirements, including details of the encryption algorithms used by the Cloud provider;
- regulatory compliance requirements, such as special protections afforded for personally identifiable information (PII);
- affirmation of data ownership stored on the Cloud service and the organization's information retrieval rights;
- system infrastructure and security standards to be maintained by the Cloud service provider, along with the organization's rights to audit compliance;
- processes for problem identification and remediation;
- change management processes for changes, updates, or new service;
- customer rights, as well as the cost to continue or discontinue using the Cloud service;
- mutual responsibility of all partners to provide notification to the other(s) in the event of data breaches.

An SLA/contract is a living document and as services and requirements change, the SLA/contract should be reassessed. Bottom line – the SLA/contract is the means by which expectations for the relationship between the organization and the Cloud provider are set.

In the US, the Government Services Agency (GSA) sponsors a program called the Federal Risk and Authorization Management Program (FedRAMP), which provides a standardized approach to the security assessment, authorization, and continuous monitoring for Cloud service providers (see *Chapter 3*, page 88). This program allows Federal agencies to select from a number of pre-approved and security-validated Cloud service providers and reduces the cost of verifying the Cloud service by using a 'do once, use many times' approach. The FedRAMP website at *www.fedramp.gov* provides a number of resources that are publicly accessible and could serve as a ready reference for organizations anywhere that are seeking secure Cloud services.

The Quick Wins

- Carefully evaluate potential Cloud service providers by reading customer reviews, as well as the Cloud provider's own documentation.
- Work with legal counsel and other knowledgeable individuals within the organization to develop a clear and comprehensive SLA/contract *prior* to engaging in use of a Cloud service provider.

Standards Mapping

STANDARD	CONTROL	SUBJECT
NIST 800-53, Security Controls for Federal Information Systems and Organizations	AC-16 (7)	Security Attributes: Consistent Attribute Interpretation
	AC-20	Use of External Information Systems
	SA-1	System and Services Acquisition Policy and Procedures
	SA-4	Acquisition Process
	SA-9	External Information System Services
	SA-13	Trustworthiness
ISO/IEC 27001:2013, Information technology – Security techniques – Information security management systems – Requirements	A.6.2.1	Identification of risks related to external parties
	A.6.2.3	Addressing security in third party agreements
	A.10.2	Third-party service delivery management
ISO/IEC 27002:2013, Information technology – Security techniques – Code of practice for information security management	15.1.1	Information security policy for supplier relationships
	15.1.2	Addressing security within supplier agreements
	15.2.1	Monitoring and review of supplier services
	15.2.2	Managing changes to supplier services

Recommendations for Additional Reading
National Institute of Standards and Technology (NIST) Special Publication (SP) 800-144. *Guidelines for Security and Privacy in Public Cloud Computing.* December 2011.

20. Deploy Sophisticated Analytic Tools

Protecting organizational information assets from the intentional or unintentional attack demands a more flexible approach. The deployment of sophisticated business intelligence tools allows organizations to continually assess data flowing into and out of the organization for warning signs that might indicate an insider threat related event.

Organizations often have a large number of disparate devices, each of which generates data in difference formats. It does little good to deploy state-of-the-art devices that collect elaborate audit logs if no tools are available to identify anomalies and misuse patterns across all the information sources. Sophisticated analytics tools are able to correlate data across multiple sources and advanced learning systems are able to look for a range of behaviors that have a high correlation to insider threat activity. This is particularly applicable to Cloud services, where visibility into the flow of traffic may provide an indicator of suspicious behavior. For example, if an organization with corporate offices in the UK using business intelligence tools identifies access into a corporate Cloud account from Russia, this might provide a clue that something unusual may be occurring with that account.

One of the primary analytic and correlation tools employed by larger organizations is a Security Information and Event Management (SIEM)* solution. A SIEM solution incorporates the following capabilities: data aggregation, correlation, alerting, dashboards, compliance monitoring, data retention, and forensic analysis. The underlying principle of a SIEM solution is a recognition that data about an organization's cybersecurity is located in multiple locations, and that the ability to see the data from a single dashboard makes it much easier to identify trends and patterns that are out of the ordinary. In order to really benefit from a SIEM solution, the organization must be able to conduct real-time monitoring and respond to events discovered by the solution. This generally means a direct relationship between the SIEM monitors and the incident response/management team.

While SIEM tools are primarily focused on information security-related events, physical security data can also be provided to the SIEM system for analysis. For example, by correlating data from the access badge system, an organization would be able to detect after-hours physical access and compare this information with the access logs to the information systems.[140]

Another requirement for an effective use of the SIEM solutions is the development of a comprehensive list of system and user behaviors that can be monitored in order to discern between normal and abnormal patterns. Misuse

---

* SIEM is pronounced like 'sim', with a silent 'e'.

detection systems are one of the information feeds that can be siphoned by the SIEM tool and used to quickly identify the 'signatures' associated with malicious insider behavior.

The Quick Wins

- Determine what should be monitored, potential log volume, and how the solution will be used before procuring any tool.
- If a SIEM is used, ensure that the solution is regularly monitored.
- Involve the incident management team in the SIEM log analysis.

Standards Mapping

STANDARD	CONTROL	SUBJECT
NIST 800-53, Security Controls for Federal Information Systems and Organizations	AU-1	Audit and Accountability Policy and Procedures
	AU-2	Audit Events
	AU-4	Audit Storage Capacity
	AU-6	Audit Review, Analysis, and Reporting
	AU-13	Monitoring for Information Disclosure
	IR-10	Integrated Information Security Analysis Team
ISO/IEC 27001:2013, Information technology – Security techniques – Information security	A.6.1.2	Information security coordination

STANDARD	CONTROL	SUBJECT
management systems – Requirements		
	A.10.10.1.	Audit logging
	A.10.10.5	Fault logging
ISO/IEC 27002:2013, Information technology – Security techniques – Code of practice for information security management	12.4	Logging and monitoring
	12.7	Information systems audit considerations

Recommendations for Additional Reading
Miller, David R.; Harris, Shon; Harper, Allen; VanDyke, Stephen; and Blask, Chris. *Security Information and Event Management (SIEM) Implementation (Network Pro Library)*. 15 November 2010. McGraw-Hill Education Publishing.

21. Secure the Supply Chain

There is another form of insider – the individual in the organization's supply chain. Supply chains are growing longer and becoming increasingly complex, and the likelihood of an insider disrupting the chain or tampering with the products has seen a dramatic increase.

A lot of organizations draw a line at the perimeter of their facility or their network. They may consider what happens 'out there' to be beyond their control. However, any time an organization depends on external entities for products or services, they incur potential risk to their mission and key service. Common supply chain concerns include the malicious use of trusted third-party relationships to gain unauthorized access to, or to harm, the organization; tampering with hardware and/or software that raises integrity issues; and breaches that involve the supplier's failure to protect sensitive information.

Before going into more detail, it is important to define what a supply chain is. Wikipedia defines the supply chain as a "system of organizations, people, activities, information and resources involve in moving a product or a service from supplier to customer. Supply chain activities involve the transformation of natural resources, raw materials, and components into a finished product that is delivered to the end customer."

Entities within the supply chain can pose unexpected risks that emerge in unexpected places. Imagine you are Verizon and a second tier provider of components for cellphone communications introduces malware that affects the operation of the phones or that allows an insider to eavesdrop on calls. Customers may complain that the phones do not work, or the insider breach may become public, and suddenly Verizon has a high-profile problem that could severely harm its reputation.

CERT UK provides several examples of supply chains being compromised. In one of these, a cyber espionage group called Dragonfly allegedly targeted organizations in Europe and North America through their supply chains. Dragonfly would compromise the websites of suppliers and replace legitimate files with files infected with malware. When an organization downloaded the files, the software would also install the malware.[141] The US DoD has identified cases of hardware delivered with malware already installed or with components that route information to external parties or nations.

The US Department of Homeland Security (DHS) has recognized that the threat to supply chains is a national security concern, as well as a concern for private customers. The supply chain provides the goods that support national infrastructures and other nations rely on the products and services in the global supply system. As such, supply chain security is a global issue that all stakeholders must work collaboratively to strengthen. "The ... security of one organization within the chain is potentially only as strong as the weakest member of that supply chain."[142]

In this vein, the White House issued a National Strategy for Global Supply Chain Security that provides an approach that is not only national in scope, but also adaptable by any organization with supply chain concerns. The recommendations include:

- Analyze the supply chain for vulnerabilities. This involves conducting a comprehensive analysis of each component in the supply chain and who is involved.

- Establish communication between the various elements within the organization involved in the supply chain. This can range from the security staff to the procurement office to the legal counsel.

- Evaluate risk by vendor. Assess and rank vendors and partners with access to the organization and/or its information systems.
- Stipulate security compliance in vendor agreements.

The Quick Wins

- Know the procurement processes from start to finish.
- Conduct thorough due diligence when choosing suppliers.
- Ensure security is included in any contract.

Standards Mapping

STANDARD	CONTROL	SUBJECT
NIST 800-53, Security Controls for Federal Information Systems and Organizations	IR-6(3)	Coordination with Supply Chain
	SA-4	Acquisition Process
	SA-9	External Information System Services
	SA-12	Supply Chain Protection
	SA-13	Trustworthiness
ISO/IEC 27001:2013, Information technology – Security techniques – Information security management systems – Requirements	A.6.2.1	Identification of risks related to external parties
	A.6.2.3	Addressing security in third party agreements
	A.10.2	Third-party service delivery management
	A.12.5.5	Outsourced software

STANDARD	CONTROL	SUBJECT
		development
ISO/IEC 27002:2013, Information technology – Security techniques – Code of practice for information security management	15.1.1	Information security policy for supplier relationships
	15.1.2	Addressing security within supplier agreements
	15.2.1	Monitoring and review of supplier services
	15.2.2	Managing changes to supplier services
ISO 28000:2007, Specification for security management systems for the supply chain	4.2	Security management policy
	4.3	Security risk assessment and planning
	4.3.5	Security management program

Recommendations for Additional Reading
Thomas, Andrew R., Editor. *Supply Chain Security: International Practices and Innovations for Moving Goods Safely and Efficiently.* 2 March 2010. Praeger Security International.

Reaction, Response, and Recovery

22. Establish an Incident Management Capability

No organization wants an incident to occur, but no organization should be without the capability to respond in the event that it does – whether or not the incident is caused by an insider threat. The primary reason for having incident management is: to enable quick, efficient recovery from security incidents; respond in a standardized and systematic manner to all types of incidents; execute all the steps in incident response and recover; prevent or minimize disruption of critical mission processes; and minimize the loss or theft of critical or sensitive assets. Although incident management is a really good idea, in many cases it is also a legal mandate. In the US, Office of Management and Budget (OMB) Publication A-130 requires all Federal organizations to develop an incident response capability to provide assistance when a security incident occurs and to share information regarding common weaknesses, threats and best practices.

The challenge of incident management is to quickly bring together a number of individuals with divergent skill sets and have them act as a cohesive team. To prepare for this challenge, an organization must develop specific policies, procedures, and guidelines. An effective response to security incidents, particularly those involving information systems, is not always a simple matter. Often, it requires a high level of technical knowledge, effective communication skills, detailed roles and responsibilities, and full coordination between organizational entities.

Since security incidents can be identified by individuals at all levels within the organization, it is important for every member of the organization to understand their roles and responsibilities. An incident response plan is an important step to establishing the organizational parameters, procedures, and responsibilities for incident response and management.

An incident can be:
1. *suspicious or confirmed activity;*
2. *attempted or successful;*
3. *deliberate or unintentional;*
4. *a measurable or potential adverse impact on the facility, information, information systems, or processes;*
5. *an explicit or implicit violation of security policy;*
6. *of possible interest to law enforcement or of forensic interest.*

The plan is a prerequisite to establishing an incident response capability or team. The actions required to rapidly and properly handle the response to an event or incident, and to later manage the incident response process, are well beyond the skills and capabilities of any single individual. A team of key players are necessary to ensure adequate execution of the plan, and this team will need both staff and management support. By identifying and formally designating specific personnel as members of an incident response 'SWAT' team in advance, the chances of a successful initial incident response are significantly improved, even when the team is an ad hoc body called together only when required to deal with an emerging incident. Suggested members of the team include at a minimum: a functional or operations expert; a technical expert, such as a system or network administrator; and a physical security expert. In addition to the members of the core incident management team, an organization should also identify additional individuals who can assist in the incident response process. The table below shows several suggested augmenting individuals and their respective roles.

Table 4: Incident Management Team

Augmenting Member	Role and Responsibilities
IT/Security Liaison	Coordinates communication between the incident management team and the security group. This individual may not have the appropriate technical expertise to serve as a primary team member, but may have the responsibility for identifying the appropriate individuals in the organization to handle specific incident aspects.
Public Relations Representative	Whether part of a formal public relations department or a designated speaker for the organization, this individual is responsible for protecting and promoting a positive image of the organization. All inquiries about the incident should be directed to this individual.
Legal Counsel	Prior to an incident, legal counsel should be consulted to provide input to the incident management plan to ensure that the organization minimizes risk when responding to an incident. It is crucial to

Augmenting Member	Role and Responsibilities
	consider the potential legal ramifications of an incident that may violate service agreements or result in a breach of information. The legal counsel should also support the public relations representative in crafting any communications with external agencies, to include law enforcement.
Management	Depending on the type, extent, impact and/or location of the incident, managers at multiple levels or across the organization might be involved in the response. A single primary management contact will assist the incident management team in identifying who needs to be notified in the specific circumstances. Management must also assist in determining the total financial and other impacts of the incident on the organization. Management should also work closely with legal counsel and public relations prior to and during the incident, to identify what can be disclosed and the level of interaction with external agencies.

Once the plan is developed, it is equally important to train the responsible individuals. The best of incident response plans can only be properly executed by trained and drilled personnel. Organizational elements at all levels should carefully review the baseline of personnel assigned key responsibilities in the plan and take forceful action to satisfy training needs rather than waiting for an incident to bring any deficiencies to light. It is also incumbent on all elements to generate and maintain an awareness of incident indicators, reporting requirements and mitigation actions contained in the plan. Email and verbal reminders, posters, and refresher training are valuable techniques in meeting this requirement.

The value of actually exercising the plan, once developed, cannot be overstated. Exercising the plan will quickly reveal areas for clarification or amendment. Procedural adjustments and hardware, software, firmware and connectivity issues that appear can be addressed, or temporary work-arounds developed to ensure successful plan implementation when an incident does surface.

The Incident Happens!

Eventually, there will come a day when an actual incident occurs. When it does, the first rule is to *remain calm*. Stress and tension caused by the incident can strain the individuals and entities involved and make even simple response actions more difficult. This can make a huge difference in how incident response is managed. In general, the response process includes two phases: the incident triage phase and the incident response management phase.

The first phase is called the incident triage phase because, much like the doctor arriving at an accident scene, a *rapid assessment* is needed to determine what *immediate actions* are required. As in all situations where the time available will be less than that believed necessary or desired, the timing of the actions may be more significant for success than the amount of time required to carry them out. Decisions will have to be made quickly based on very sketchy information, and by the people on the scene, but remember – inexperienced personnel should take *no* actions until the incident response experts arrive. *Figure 33* illustrates the actions taken in this first phase.

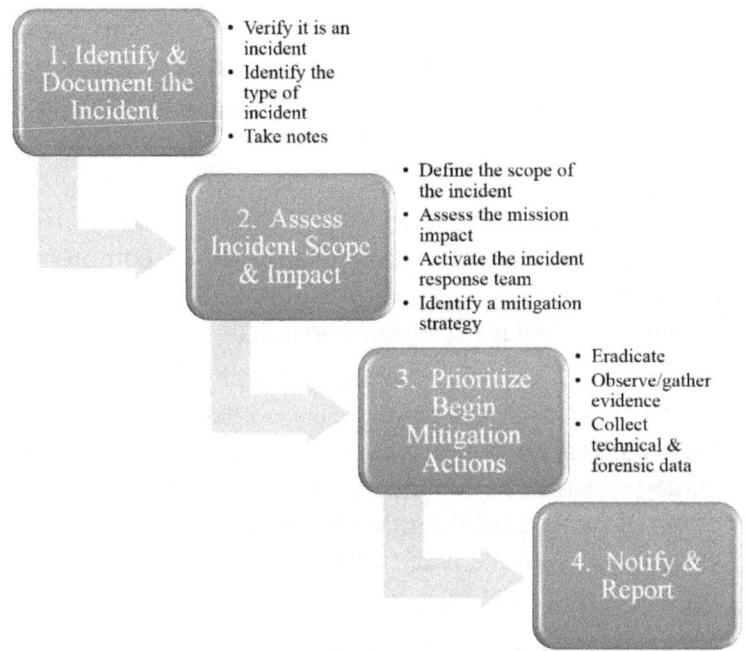

Figure 33: Incident triage phases

One of the most important actions during the triage phase is the prioritization of the mitigation actions, particularly since the organization rarely has the resources or the expertise to address all actions immediately and completely. In developing recommended courses of action to address the impacts of an incident; the following priority list should be used to determine the order in which mitigation actions will be taken:

1. Priority one – protect human life and people's safety. Mitigation of incidents that threaten human life or safety always will take precedence over all other considerations.

2. Priority two – protect corporate critical assets, intellectual property and/or classified data. Take steps to mitigate incident impacts that might compromise the facility or classified and/or sensitive systems, networks or sites.

3. Priority three – protect other official and sensitive physical assets and data from destruction or compromise, including managerial data that would be costly in terms of resources to replace if lost or corrupted.

4. Priority four – prevent damage to physical assets and information systems (e.g. loss or alteration of system files, damage to disk drives, etc.). Steps taken to mitigate damage to the facility and its systems can avoid costly down time degrading mission performance and speed system and data recovery efforts.

5. Priority five – minimize disruption of computing business processes. The decision on which mitigation actions to take in order to minimize service disruptions can be difficult. In some cases, it may be necessary and more advantageous to close the facility, shut a system down or disconnect it from a network rather than to risk long-term data or systems damage. Sites will have to evaluate the trade-offs between a shutdown and keeping the organization operational. The decision to remain operational and risk potential damage may be required to monitor and observe how the incident evolves, or may be required by service agreements governing the operation of site critical systems. However, if the damage and/or scope of an incident become so extensive that they approach the priority one or two criteria above, service agreements may have to be overridden.

An exceptionally crucial aspect of the incident response process is to inform management that an incident is underway or has occurred. Reporting should be done as securely as possible in order to avoid undue attention and the possible disruption of the incident response process. In many cases, management will designate a specific staff expert, perhaps a public relations expert, to assist in managing and providing reports on the incident response status, particularly to external entities.

The next phase of an incident is the response management phase. This phase is focused on taking control of the ongoing situation and making a more in-depth assessment of the incident. The decisions in this phase will be made based on much more information, and by the full organizational management structure. By this point, support from the incident response capability will also be available. The focus will be on adjusting procedures and activities to maintain or restore normal operations, and to identify and eliminate the vulnerabilities that made the probe or attack successful. The four steps in this phase are illustrated in *Figure 34*.

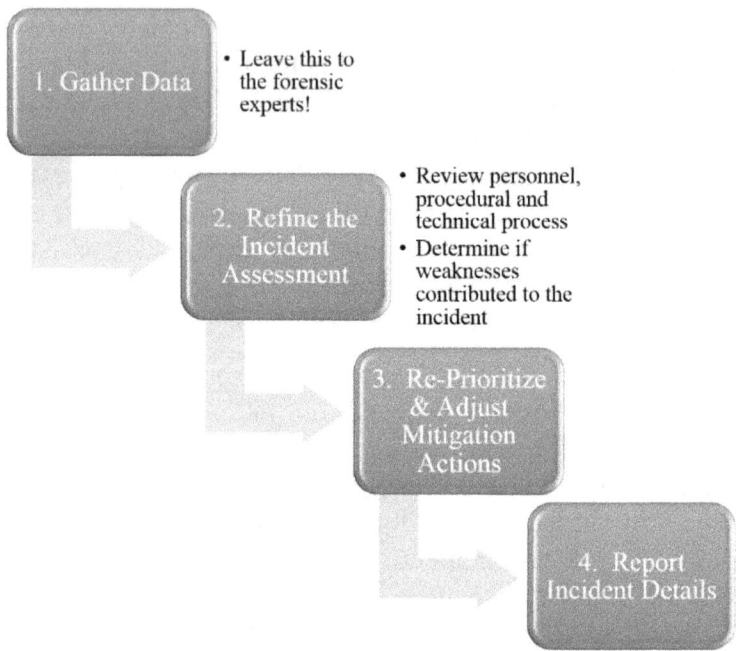

Figure 34: The incident management phase

For many companies, an incident – insider threat-related or not – can cause a public media crisis. For these organizations, having a plan for managing the public response is critical. The main rule is this: don't handle a public relations incident by simply pretending it does not exist. For highly public incidents, such as the Sony data breach or the hack of the US Office of Personnel Management (OPM), customers want the organization to acknowledge that an incident occurred, and to tell them what cause the incident, and what is being done to prevent similar incidents in the future. An organization entrusted with sensitive information has a responsibility to protect that information. Be aware that a headline in the newspaper, or even more so on national news stations, can be potentially more destructive than the incident itself.

After the incident has been resolved, a *post-mortem* should be conducted to learn from the experience and, if necessary, update procedures, policies and plans. The following items should be examined:

- How the incident started?
- Which vulnerabilities were exploited?
- How access was gained?
- How the organization and the incident response team became aware of the incident?
- How the incident was resolved?
- Whether existing procedures were adequate or require updating?
- Whether vulnerabilities still need to be closed?
- Whether notification and/or alert procedures were adequate?
- What were the direct and indirect impacts of the incident?

Complete documentation of the above items should be used to develop lessons learned, input to training, revisions or additions to existing policy and procedures, updates to the incident response plan, revisions to service level agreements (SLAs), and requirements for facility or information system upgrades.

Prevention is Better than Cure

There is a clear benefit in being able to respond effectively to a security incident. However, there are both direct and indirect benefits if an organization can demonstrate that it is able to detect or deter an incident, as well as provide effective responses. In security, and especially when considering insider threats, prevention is better than cure. While it is impossible to prevent all security incidents, a number of actions can be proactively taken by the incident management team to minimize the number and impact:

- Clearly establish, publish, and enforce security policies and procedures. As discussed in *Chapter 3*, many security incidents are accidently initiated by individuals who have not followed or do not understand the procedures.

- Get management support for security policies and for the incident management procedures.

- Research and routinely apply appropriate system patches and anti-malware software updates.

- Routinely assess vulnerabilities in the environment – not only in the information systems.

- Conduct initial and continuing training for the members of the incident management team.

- Routinely monitor and analyze network traffic and overall system performance.

- Routinely check all audit logs and logging mechanisms, including the operating system logs, application logs, user activity logs, and intrusion detection logs.

- Verify backup and restore procedures. Be aware of where backups are stored and who has access. Know and test the procedures for data restoration and system discovery.

The Quick Wins

- Develop and test an organizationally-specific incident response plan.
- Identify a team of experts to act as a 'rapid reaction force' in the event of an incident and ensure that each member is aware of and trained in their respective role.
- Ensure a trained public relations expert handles any interactions with the media in order to manage any published information.

Standards Mapping

STANDARD	CONTROL	SUBJECT
NIST 800-53, Security Controls for Federal Information Systems and Organizations	IR-1	Incident Response Policy and Procedures
	IR-4	Incident Handling
	IR-5	Incident Monitoring
	IR-6	Incident Reporting
	IR-8	Incident Response Plan
	IR-9	Information Spillage Response
	IR-10	Integrated Information Security Analysis Team
ISO/IEC 27001:2013, Information technology – Security techniques – Information security management systems – Requirements	A.13	Management of information security incidents and improvements
	A.13.2.1	Responsibilities and procedures
ISO/IEC 27002:2013, Information technology – Security techniques –	`16	Information security incident management

STANDARD	CONTROL	SUBJECT
Code of practice for information security management		
	16.1	Management of information security incidents and improvements

Recommendations for Additional Reading
O'Toole, Darren. *Incident Management for I.T. Departments... in 10 Easy Steps*. 3 April 2015. Amazon Digital Services LLC.
Mitchell, Stewart. *How to Survive a Data Breach: A Pocket Guide*. 17 February 2009. IT Governance Publishing.
Krausz, Michael. *Managing Information Security Breaches: Studies from Real Life*. 29 January 2015. IT Governance Publishing.

23. Protect Forensic Evidence

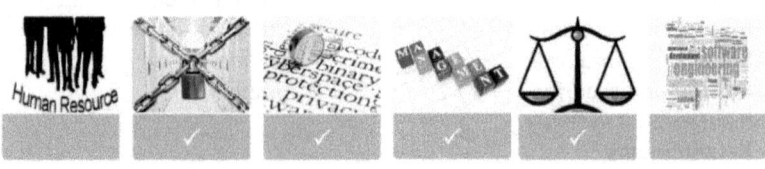

Today is the day an organization discovers that an insider threat has been active within its information systems, and the individual is immediately terminated. At 8:30 am on

Wednesday, the employee is notified he is being let go and is escorted by a security guard as he cleans out his desk and is then escorted off the premises. As soon as he is gone, the IT staff retrieve the employee's computer and begin to dig around inside looking for incriminating evidence and copying any potentially compromised documents and files to a thumb drive. Only after all this has occurred, do they think to call in the forensic examiner. What the organization has now created is a forensic expert's worst nightmare. The evidence may have been compromised, if not outright destroyed.

In the case of an insider threat incident, or any other for that matter, the organization may want to pursue legal action against the wrongdoer(s). In order to preserve this option, it is crucial to protect any evidence. Only an individual skilled in forensics should conduct any investigation of the crime scene, whether it is based on access to the facility or access to the information systems.

An unfortunate side effect of the proliferation of TV shows, like CSI, is that everyone has become a 'forensic expert'. The result is that the real forensic examiner is now frequently confronted with a situation where the evidence that must be collected and preserved in order for it to be legally admissible in a court of law is irreversibly damaged and inadmissible.

The primary aim of any forensic investigation is to recover some form of evidence, or objective data that has relevance to the examination. Regardless of the type of incident, the investigators will essentially follow the forensic process illustrated in *Figure 35*, although the techniques might be different: identification, or determination of the type of incident; preparation, or identifying and positioning the proper tools, techniques, search warrants; preservation, or protection of the crime scene so evidence is not lost or compromised; acquisition, or the process of collecting and documenting the evidence; analysis, which is the evaluation of the evidence collected; and reporting, or the production of an evidence package.

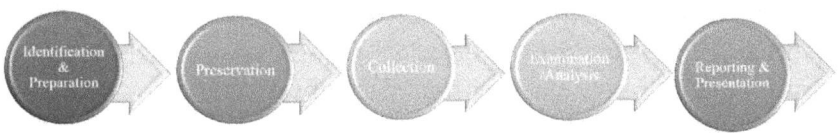

Figure 35: Forensic investigation process

Digital forensics is a branch of forensics that involves the recovery and analysis of content found in digital form, often as a result of some form of computer incident or crime. The digital forensic investigation process generally follows all the same steps as any other forensic examination.

Digital forensics has several unique qualities based on the very nature of the data – it is easily modified, even just by accessing it. In order to protect the evidence, organizations should not engage in do-it-yourself forensics. This type of forensics has permeated a number of organizations, either because of cost considerations and/or the lack of skilled forensic personnel on their internal teams.

The biggest pitfalls in using home-grown IT staff instead of forensic experts in the case of a digital incident include:

- a weak or even non-existent chain of custody;
- unintentional spoilage or tampering with the evidence;

- overlooked evidence;
- lack of objectivity;
- use of inferior tools and methods;
- inability to demonstrate that the staff is properly trained and certified.

Another problem is that it is the general user that is often the first person to become aware of a security incident that requires investigation. For these users, there are four simple rules to follow:

1. *Do not* turn off the computer if it is on.
2. *Do* isolate the system, disconnect it from the network and secure the physical area.
3. *Do not* allow the IT staff to execute any searches on the system – improper investigation will compromise or even destroy evidence.
4. *Do* contact the incident response team and let an experienced forensic expert take over.

The Quick Wins

- Provide every user with a deskside incident response checklist with dos and don'ts and a list of who to contact.
- Include training in the protection of forensic evidence in the general security training.

Standards Mapping

STANDARD	CONTROL	SUBJECT
NIST 800-53, Security Controls for Federal Information Systems and Organizations	IR-2	Incident Response Training
	IR-7	Incident Response Assistance
	IR-10	Integrated Information Security Analysis Team
ISO/IEC 27001:2013, Information technology – Security techniques – Information security management systems – Requirements	A.8.2.2	Awareness, education and training
	A.13.1	Reporting information security events and weaknesses
	A.13.2	Management of information security incidents and improvements
	A.13.2.3	Collection of evidence
ISO/IEC 27002:2013, Information technology – Security techniques – Code of practice for information security management	16.1	Management of information security incidents

Recommendations for Additional Reading
The Open University. *Introduction to computer forensics and investigations*. 16 September 2015. Open University Press.

Clarke, Nathan. *Computer Forensics: A Pocket Guide.* 6
April 2010. IT Governance Publishing.

24. Implement and Test Secure Backup and Recovery Processes

Recent headlines about high-profile insider threat events have brought increasing attention to the topic, but comparatively little is published about the role of secure backup and recovery in addressing the problem. Backup and recovery are just not 'sexy', but their role could not be more important.

The truth is that, despite all of the precautions an organization may take, nothing can completely rule out the possibility of an insider attack. So, while prevention may be the first line of defense, having good backup and restoration practices in the event of an insider threat event may significantly decrease or even eliminate the months or years of effort that are sometimes required to reconstruct information assets.

What exactly does information backup mean? Essentially, all digital information with value to the organization should be copied – or backed up to – secure storage media on a regular basis. Backups enable the recovery of data, systems and applications in the event of a natural disaster, system drive failure, data entry error, system operations error or violation by an insider threat. They should be designed to facilitate the restoration and execution of essential business functions during any emergency or situation that disrupts normal operations. Backups can use a variety of media, such as tape drives, removable cartridges, CDs/ DVDs, external hard drives, network storage, and Cloud storage. The type of media is largely determined by the amount of information to be backed up and the frequency of the backup activities.

In addition to the media, a combination of backup methodologies can be used depending on the information system configuration and asset recovery requirements. The frequency and extend of the backup should be based on the importance of the information and the information owner's level of risk tolerance. The various system backup methodologies are:

- Full – a full backup captures all files on the system selected for backup. The time required for a full backup can be extensive. Also, full backups can be storage intensive.

- Incremental – an incremental backup captures any files that were created or changed since the last backup. Incremental backups are a more efficient use of storage media and the time required for the backup is reduced. The drawback of incremental backups is that recovery may require media from different backup operations. For example, if the last full backup was conducted a week ago and one file changed each day, then the full backup media *plus* each day's incremental backup would be needed to restore all of the content.

- Differential – a differential backup stores any content created or modified since the last *full* backup. Although a differential backup takes less time than a full backup, it does require more time and storage than an incremental backup.

Based on the criticality of the data, the backup media may require both onsite and offsite storage. When making a determination regarding offsite storage, in particular, there are a number of considerations, including (1) distance from the organization and the likelihood of the storage site being affected by the same event as the primary site; (2) length of time required to retrieve the backups from data storage; (3) security of the offsite location for both the site and the personnel; (4) environmental and structural conditions of the offsite location; and (5) cost of moving the media to the facility, operational and storage fees, and disaster response/recovery services.

A backup and recovery plan establishes the guidelines and procedures for the process based on organizational requirements. The importance of a backup and restoration plan cannot be overstated. The backup section of the plan should define the procedures for backing up baseline configurations*, servers, the most recent system and user data, and testing the restore process for each of the above environments. Additionally, the plan should include who is responsible for performing the backups, the periodic backup schedule, and instructions for securing the backup files and media. A policy outline for the backup portion of the plan might look like this:

- A standard installation image for each type of workstation shall be made for the quick and easy restoration of computers in the event of a unit failure.

---

* The baseline configuration is the configuration of the asset/information system at a point in time, which serves as the basis for defining and controlling change.

- All unique installations shall be imaged upon completion of their build process for the quick and easy restoration of computers in the event of a unit failure.

- All servers shall be imaged upon completion of initial configuration, and re-imaged following any significant changes in software arrangements.

- All network devices (defined as servers, CD image servers, or NAS) and unique workstations (defined as developer or programmer computers) shall be included in the following backup scheme:
  - Monday – full backup after normal working hours are completed
  - Tuesday-Thursday – differential backup after normal working hours are completed
  - Friday – full backup after normal working hours are completed
  - Saturday-Sunday – incremental backup after normal working hours are completed
  - Daily – database backups using Oracle backup agent to NAS and designated storage on the BDC for redundancy.

- Tapes shall be rotated in sets as defined in Step 4 above, with weekly sets stored in the fire safe. On a monthly basis, tapes shall be rotated from the safe to an off-site storage unit.

- A minimum of three months' backups shall be maintained off-site.

- Once a quarter, sample sets of data shall be restored from tape to verify data integrity and IS&T's ability to recover information.

- The maximum permissible downtime on account of data loss should comply with the following scheme:

- Application software – 1 working day (WD)
- Server application software – 1 WD
- Workstation applications (critical) – 1 WD
- Workstation applications (non-critical) – 5 WD
- Oracle database information (critical) – 2 hours
- Oracle database information (non-critical) – 1WD
- Lessons or teaching presentations for the current day – 15 minutes
- Lessons or teaching presentations for other days – 1 WD
- Personal data or e-mail (critical) – 1 WD
- Personal data or e-mail (non-critical) – 5 WD.

- Regular IS&T training shall occur on data backup and recovery methods to coincide with the quarterly recovery tests.

- Data redundancy shall follow the following basic scheme:
  - Raid-0 on all server OS drives (two OS drives per server)
  - Raid-5 on all server data stores.

The restoration portion of the plan should define the recovery and rollback process, which allows an organization to return to an earlier state. This portion of the plan should define just how much downtime an organization can tolerate, provide a list of the most critical systems, and identify processes for recovering data. The recovery process may involve restoring data from backup media, switching to redundant systems or servers, or rolling back* to a previous configuration. Bottom line – if data

---

* Rollback means returning the system or production environment to a state before changes were made – or before an insider executed an attack.

assets cannot be restored from a backup, it is not really a backup at all. One of the worst cases I have seen involved an organization that had more than eight years of stored backups. All was well until the day the main servers crashed. In all those years, the data restoration process had not been tested even once – and to its dismay, the organization discovered that it had eight full years of empty folders!

Backing up information is not the only important thing. It's equally important to protect the backups, particularly when using third-party providers for the backup services, which may also involve off-site storage of backup media. A backup must be at least as secure as the data being backed up, because a compromised backup is just as bad as a compromised primary data asset. By their very nature, backups introduce additional threats to an organization's data assets. With each additional copy of data, the risk of unauthorized access or compromise is increased. The protection requirements will vary greatly based on the nature of the information being backup up. Personnel records and health files might be much more sensitive than files from a construction company, and certainly, any classified backup must have appropriate protection.

More and more organizations are taking advantage of the Cloud for their backup and recovery solutions, and Cloud service providers are multiplying like rabbits. When looking at Cloud backup services, consider the following:

- complexity of any self-service interfaces and processes for recovery from a Cloud service;
- availability of the Cloud service staff required for recovery and/or restoration;

- stability of the Cloud connectivity (what happens if a lack of connectivity hampers recovery);
- possibility of data corruption or compromise;
- protection for data residing within the Cloud.

Data backups in the Cloud can be protected with a few simple considerations. Data should be encrypted from the time it leaves the organization and remain encrypted for the entire time it is stored in any given Cloud architecture. Use an agentless architecture that does not require any pieces of backup software to be installed on organizational servers and devices. Verify that the Cloud provider has at least one redundant data storage center in a geographically separate location and that this location is not at high risk of a natural disaster. Finally, the organization should know where the data resides at any given point in time.

The Quick Wins

- Develop a formal data backup and recovery plan.
- Control access to the online backup data as well as the physical media used for the backups.
- Have redundant copies of backups.
- Periodically test restoration from the backup media.
- Ensure backup accountability and security is addressed in all contracts with third-party vendors providing backup services.
- Consider encrypting the backup media, especially when copies are maintained by a third-party vendor at an off-site location.

Standards Mapping

STANDARD	CONTROL	SUBJECT
NIST 800-53, Security Controls for Federal Information Systems and Organizations	CP-6	Alternate Storage Site
	CP-9	Information System Backup
	CP-10	Information System Recovery and Reconstitution
ISO/IEC 27001:2013, Information technology – Security techniques – Information security management systems – Requirements	10.5.1	Back-Up
ISO/IEC 27002:2013, Information technology – Security techniques – Code of practice for information security management	12.3.1	Information backup
	15.1.2	Addressing security within supplier agreements
	15.2.1	Monitoring and review of supplier services

Recommendations for Additional Reading
Preston, W. Curtis. *Backup & Recovery: Inexpensive Backup Solutions for Open Systems.* 13 January 2007. O'Reilly Media Publishing.
Thejendra, BS. *Disaster Recovery and Business Continuity: A Quick Guide for Small Organizations and*

> *Busy Executives, 3rd Edition.* 30 January 2014. IT Governance Publishing.

Insider Threat 'Worst Practices'

Throughout this chapter, the focus has been on best practices and quick wins. But before we leave, it's equally important to look at ten of the 'worst practices' identified by Bunn and Sagan,[143] as well as a couple more developed by the author, and learn to avoid them. These worst practices were derived from past mistakes and are intended to provide some lessons learned – the hard way!

Worst Practice #1: Assuming that Insider Threats are Not in My Organization (NIMO)

Organizations that assume their staff are part of a carefully screened elite, such as government intelligence agencies and the banking industry, often fall prey to the belief that insider threat happens to others and never to themselves.

Worst Practice #2: Assuming That Background Investigations Are Sufficient to Weed Out the Insider Threat

Edward Snowden provides the perfect demonstration of why you should *not* assume that a security clearance and a background check will effectively weed out potential insider threats. Snowden had been investigated and vetted by some of the most secure US institutions, such as the NSA. This is directly linked to the NIMO phenomenon above and – at least until recently – was a very widespread belief.

There are two reasons why this is a worst practice: (1) Background checks, even those conducted by highly restrictive agencies, are often incomplete and ineffective, particularly when used as the sole criteria for trust; and (2) just like Snowden, even those employees vetted as trustworthy can turn into insider threats later on. Polygraphs as a basis for complete trust are equally ineffective. One of the greatest FBI insider threats, Aldrich Ames, passed his polygraph examinations. So, no matter how in-depth a background investigation may be, the lesson learned is to implement an insider threat training program and maintain a program of continuous evaluation of all employees – particularly those with trusted access.

Worst Practice #3: Assuming that Red Flags Will Be Promptly Noticed and Properly Recognized and Addressed

Chapter 2 provides an in-depth discussion of character traits and behavior patterns that might indicate the presence of an insider threat. Yet even with knowledge of these indicators, most organizations will tend to ignore red flags or be reluctant to act on them. For example, consider the shooting incident at Fort Hood, Texas, where US Army Major Nidal Hasan killed thirteen soldiers and wounded more than 30 individuals who were in a deployment preparation center. For quite a while prior to the shooting, Major Hasan had made his views about radicalization and his devotion to Sharia law well known. He had even gone so far as to engage in communications with a known terrorist. Yet no one took action on these very obvious red flags. If such clear signals can be ignored, how successful will most organizations be at recognizing and acting on much more subtle signals, such as those outlined in *Chapter 2*?

One of the primary problems is the lack of sharing across organizational elements. The case of Major Hasan is an excellent example of this problem, too. In Hasan's case, the various Joint Terrorist Task Forces (JTTFs) monitoring his emails did not communicate, nor did they share the information they had detected with the US Army organization where Major Hasan was assigned. Finally, "a junior Department of Defense official in the Washington JTTF, after reviewing the positive OERs, made the tragic and controversial decision that Hasan's email conversations with al-Awlaki were just part of a research project; he therefore did not feel the need to pass on the intelligence reports to Hasan's superior officers."[144]

Worst Practice #4: Assuming that Insider Threats Will Not Conspire

Most insider threats are loners. However, it is incorrect to assume that they will always act alone. This has become increasingly evident in recent terrorist-based insider incidents, such as the shooting that took place on 2 December 2015 in San Bernardino, CA. In this case, Syed Farook and Tashfeen Malik shot and killed 14 people and injured a further 22 in an attack on employees of the Department of Public Health (DPH) during a training event and Christmas holiday party. Farook, an employee of the DPH, and Malik, were a married couple who became radicalized and conspired together to commit a terrorist act. The lesson here is that insider threats can and may conspire, and organizations should include approaches for identifying possible conspiracies in their insider threat programs.

Worst Practice #5: Relying on a Single Protective Measures and Boundary Defense

When considering appropriate insider threat detection and deterrence, organizations often place a high level of trust in certain elements of their security program to the neglect of others. This may be take the form of a reliance on their physical security perimeter or a belief that their perimeter firewall will protect their information system assets from compromise. Insider threats, however, quickly become aware of weaknesses in the security layers and will seek the path of least resistance.

In the case of Private Bradley (Chelsea) Manning, a number of security policies were ignored, allowed her to download classified documents onto a CD while inside a security facility. Manning quickly ascertained that security monitoring of removable media was lacking. The guards did not check incoming and outgoing staff for media, despite the existence of policies prohibiting the transport of personally-owned media into the security facility. There were rules against the burning of any files onto a CD, but these were not enforced. As a result, Manning was able to copy thousands of sensitive and classified files and provide WikiLeaks and its owner, Julien Assange, with what might be considered one of the largest collections of stolen state secrets in US history. The lesson learned here is that a single security measure is not sufficient and that no security measure is sufficient if not followed.

Worst Practice #6: Ignoring the Impact of Organizational Culture

A culture of security begins with a comprehensive risk assessment and flows down from top management. A lack of strategic security planning, combined with a feeble or uneven implementation of security policies and procedures, contributes to an organizational culture that is much more susceptible to security breaches and insider threats. A shift towards a viable security culture must start at the top, with the senior management team engaging in strategic security thinking. They must then foster the same thinking throughout the organization in the form of security values that they themselves adhere to. General Eugene Habiger, former Commander in Chief to the US Strategic Command, put it this way: "Good security is 20% hardware and 80% culture."[145]

Dissatisfaction with the organization is a proven ingredient in the development or an insider threat. A good security culture can go a long way towards preventing employee disgruntlement. A poor, or negative, culture of security – or one that is too casual, disorganized, or even unethical in its values and practices – will equally adversely affect employee satisfaction and performance. It lowers employee self-confidence by diminishing their sense of importance; morale shrinks in an atmosphere that lacks strong security values.

Worst Practice #7: Paying no Attention to the Fact that Insider Threats Know about the Organization's Security Weaknesses

Insider threats are observant; they will soon identify the security weaknesses in their environment, particularly since many insider threats are in trust positions that give them the opportunity to understand the organization's security measures and any associated vulnerabilities. Again, Private Manning provides an excellent example to illustrate this point. Snowden is yet another example of an individual in a high position of trust and access, who quickly recognized which vulnerabilities in his organization were most easily exploitable. As a system administrator, he had the keys to the IT kingdom and he used his privileges to gain unauthorized access to files, circumvent technologies designed to prevent file transfers to external media, and then erase his steps after successfully downloading gigabytes of files onto removable media.

CMU SEI research into insider threat repeatedly revealed that the success of the insider activities depended largely on the insider's knowledge and exploitation of existing organizational weaknesses. There is a lesson learned here: in order to effectively counter this element of the insider threat, organizations must examine themselves with the mindset of an 'exploiter', and then develop security measures that would be effective against the range of possible access avenues identified. Traditional, or unimaginative, security countermeasures will never be sufficient to fully defend against or deter a determined insider threat.

Worst Practice #8: Assuming that Security Rules Actually Take Precedence Over Day-to-Day Operations

Almost everyone has worked for an organization that has well-written security policies and known procedures, but where the rules have been bent to meet a deadline, to avoid the inconvenience, or to keep production moving. While the policies say comply with security, the actual day-to-day work environment may instead convey that "Every hour an employee spends following the letter of security procedures is an hour not spent on activities more likely to result in a promotion or raise."[146]

In some cases, the security requirements are so complex or onerous that employees will either violate them unintentionally or will intentionally bypass the rules. How often have you heard 'never write down your password', even though at the same time your organization demands a 15-character, complex, randomly generated password that is changed every 30 days? Such complex rules are often an invitation for finding a way around the rule. The result: rather than running the risk of forgetting the password and being locked out of the system, staff write it down and store it in a 'secure' wallet!

Organizations need to find the critical balance between security rules that are essential and those that are simply overly burdensome and actually contribute very little to mitigating the real security issues. Government organizations are often the worst offenders – every security incident generally results in more rules being added, rather than a serious re-evaluation of existing security measures and their implementation. According to Dr. Roger G. Johnson, head of the Vulnerability Assessment Team (VAT) at Argonne National Labs, "In any large organization, at least 30% of the security rules, policies, and procedures are pointless, absurd, ineffective, or actually undermine security (by wasting energy and resources, by creating cynicism about security, and/or by driving behaviors that were not anticipated."

Worst Practice #9: Ignoring the Threat from the Naïve or Unintentional Insider

The intentional, malicious insider threat may pose a significant danger to organizations, but it would be unwise to neglect the threat posed by the naïve or unintentional insider. As indicated in *Chapter 3*, these individuals are either unaware of the rules or violate them with 'good' intentions. Even the most comprehensive definitions of an insider threat tend to ignore this type of insider without malicious intent.

Quite frequently, this type of insider threat stems from poor judgement, lack of knowledge, or misplaced intent. "The insider threat from careless or complacent employees and contractors exceeds the threat from malicious insiders (though the latter is not negligible) ... This is partially, though not totally, due to the fact that careless or complacent insiders often unintentionally help nefarious outsiders."[147]

This is one area where in-depth security screenings and background checks are largely ineffective. These methods may detect a potential malicious insider, but they are largely unsuccessful in identifying individuals who are naïve or possess poor judgment. Having a viable culture of security and ensuring that security rules are reasonable and implementable will go a long way towards minimizing the likelihood of the unintentional insider causing a breach.

Worst Practice #10: Focusing on the Technical 'Silver Bullet'

There is a strong temptation to rely heavily on the technical 'silver bullets'. It is easy for organizations to view the prevention, detection and response to insider threats as an IT problem. In contrast to approaches that focus on understanding challenges from people and processes, technology has substance and is must less subject to interpretation. Unfortunately, the idea that technology can provide a solution to the persistent and ever-evolving array of insider threats is one of the most persistent myths of security – it often manifests as a belief that a better firewall, intrusion detection, monitoring, and/or automated assessments will ensure a secure environment. While technology is certainly one element, perhaps even a critical element, organizations should not be single-mindedly focused on finding that one technology that will solve their problems.

True insider threat prevention, detection and response requires a layered set of solutions that begin with management commitment, are codified in policies and procedures, supported by good personnel security awareness, and aided by technology implementations.

Recommendations for Additional Reading
Stefanek, George L. *Information Security Best Practices: 205 Basic Rules.* 2 April 2002. Butterworth-Heinemann Publishing.
Calder, Alan. *Implementing Information Security based on ISO 27001/ISO 27002 (Best Practice), 2nd Edition.* 31 July 2009. Van Haren Publishing.
Greene, Sari. *Security Program and Policies: Principles and Practices, 2nd Edition.* 29 March 2014. Pearson IT Certification.

CHAPTER 7: FINAL THOUGHTS

When eating an elephant take one bite at a time. –
*Creighton Adams[148]

This book can only provide a beginning to addressing insider threat. This is a problem that will continue to evolve as technologies increase both the amount of data available and the access to that data. In order to be effective, we need to understand the insider 'gone bad' and capitalize on the outcomes of continuing research, such as that being done by CMU SEI in the US and the CPNI in the UK.

If there is only one conceptual take-away from this book, it is that the insider threat comes in diverse and complex forms, that those involved can have a multitude of motives, and that the common, often unknown or undetected, organizational flaws make the insider threat a difficult problem to address.

The greatest enemy of effective action is complacency, combined with the belief that insider threat 'does not happen here' and the security measures in place are sufficient. Another problem is the perception that the sheer difficulty of understanding the insider threat and determining appropriate countermeasures is absolutely overwhelming and thus it cannot be effectively addressed.

So, how do you 'eat the elephant' that is insider threat? As the old joke suggests – one bite at a time.

---

* Creighton Abrams was a US Army general who led military operations during the Vietnam War. The main battle tank of the US Army, the M1 Abrams, was named after him.

Source: Microsoft Office Free Clip Art

Figure 36: How do you eat an elephant?

Everyone has heard this saying, but too often we fail to take this lesson to heart. If the elephant, also known as the insider threat, is viewed as one enormous, complicated obstacle, it may lead organizations to freeze up and cease to act at all.

Instead of looking at the insider threat problem in this way, it is much better to break it down into its individual parts and address them one at a time. Further, it is worthwhile to consider the prevention, detection, and response to insider threat as a journey, not a destination. Get started, form a core team, conduct your risk assessment and analysis, determine a way ahead, and then take the first step on the way to the detection, prevention and recovery from insider threats.

END NOTES

[1] "Resources: Top Issues: Insider Threat." *National Counterintelligence and Security Center*. Accessed November 21, 2015. *http://ncsc.gov/ issues/ithreat/index.html.*

[2] Thornberry, Mac. "Head in the Sand." *Search Quotes*. Accessed November 5, 2015. *www.searchquotes.com/quotation/And_to_stick_our_head_in_the_sand_ and_pretend_that_we_are_somehow_safer_if_we_do_not_know_or_to_ pret/189493/.*

[3] Mann, Herbie. "Herbie Mann Quotes." *Brainy Quote*. Accessed October 13, 2015. *www.brainyquote.com/quotes/quotes/h/ herbiemann305167.html.*

[4] Cole E. Addressing the insider threat with NetIQ Operational Change Control Solutions. *www.bitpipe.com/detail/RES/1155054635_181.html*

[5] Charney, David L. M.D. "True Psychology of the Insider Spy." *Intelligence Journal of U.S. Intelligence Studies*, no. Fall/Winter 2010 (n.d.): 47–54.

[6] Threat Quotes. *Search Quotes*. Accessed 15 January 2016. *Search Quotes. www.searchquotes.com/search/Threat/3/*

[7] Contos, Brian T. *Enemy at the Water Cooler*. Rockland, MA: Syngress Publishing, Inc., 2006.

[8] Keeney, Michelle, Eileen Kowalski, Dawn Capelli, Andrew P. Moore, Timothy Shimeall, and Stephanie Rogers. "Insider Threat Study: Computer System Sabotage: Critical Infrastructure Sectors." Carnegie Mellon Software Engineering Institute, May 2005. *http://resources.sei.cmu.edu/library/asset-view.cfm?assetID=51934.*

[9] Gelles, Dr. Michael, and Dr. Jesse Goldhammer. "From Bricks and Mortar to Bits and Bytes: A History and Future of Insider Threat." presented at the RSA Conference 2015, San Francisco, CA, April 20, 201AD. *www.rsaconference.com/events/us15/agenda/sessions/1668/ bricks-and-mortar-to-bits-and-bytes-a-history-and.*

[10] Noonan, Thomas, and Edmund Archuleta. "The Insider Threat to Critical Infrastructures." The National Infrastructure Advisory Council, April 8, 2008. *www.dhs.gov/xlibrary/assets/niac/niac_insider_threat_ to_critical_infrastructures_study.pdf.*

[11] Magklaras, G.B., and S.M. Furnell. "Insider Threat Prediction Tool: Evaluating the Probability of IT Misuse." *Computers & Security* 21, no. 1 (2002): 62–78.

[12] Silowash, George, Dawn Capelli, Andrew P. Moore, Randall Trzeciak, Timothy Shimeall, and Lori Flynn. "Common Sense Guide to Mitigating Insider Threat, 4th Edition." Technical Report. Carnegie Mellon Software Engineering Institute, December 2012. *www.sei.cmu.edu*.

[13] "SpectorSoft 2014 Insider Threat Survey." Vero Beach, FL: SpectorSoft, 2014. *www.spectorsoft.com*.

[14] "Oxford Dictionaries," n.d. *www.oxforddictionaries.com/us/*.

[15] Gaudin, Sharon. "Ex-UBS Employee Sentenced to 97 Months in Jail." *Information Week*, December 13, 2006, sec. Software//Enterprise Applications. *www.informationweek.com/ex-ubs-systems-admin-sentenced-to-97-months-in-jail/d/d-id/1049873*.

[16] Oxford Dictionaries.

[17] "WHITE PAPER - What Is the Insider Threat." The Security Company, January 2013. *www.thesecurityco.com/media/40631/Whitepaper-insider-threat_January2013.pdf*.

[18] U.S. Office of Thrift Supervision. *Examination Handbook on Fraud and Insider Abuse*. Vol. Section 360. Regulatory Bulletin 37-54. U.S. Departent of the Treasury, 2010.

[19] Ibid., 360.6.

[20] Ibid., 360.6.

[21] Ibid., 360.7.

[22] Hamilton, Robert. "The 'Frenemy' Within - Insider Theft of Ntellectual Property." *Voice of Symantec*, February 6, 2013. *www.symantec.com/connect/blogs/frenemy-within-insider-theft-intellectual-property*.

[23] Ibid.

[24] Collins, Matt. "Theft of Intellectual Property by Insiders." *Insider Threat Blog*, December 18, 2013. *https://insights.sei.cmu.edu/insider-threat/2013/12/-theft-of-intellectual-property-by-insiders.html*.

[25] Moore, Andrew P., Dawn Capelli, Thomas C. Caron, Eric D. Shaw, Derrick Spooner, and Randall Trzeciak. "A Preliminary Model of Insider Theft of Intellectual Property," June 2011. *http://resources.sei.cmu.edu/library/asset-view.cfm?assetID=9855*.

[26] Collins. "Theft of Intellectual Property by Insiders."

[27] Collins, Matt, Derrick Spooner, Dawn Capelli, Andrew P. Moore, and Randall Trzeciak. "Spotlight On: Insider Theft of Intellectual

Property Inside the United States Involving Foreign Governments or Organizations." Technical Note, May 2013. *www.sei.cmu.edu*.

[28] "The Insider Threat: An Introduction to Detecting and Deterring an Insider Spy." U.S. Department of Justice, October 31, 2012.

[29] Stamati-Koromina, Veroniki, Christos K. Georgiadis, Christos Ilioudis, Richard Overill, and Demosthenes Stamatis. "Insider Threats in Corporate Environments: A Case Study for Data Leakage Protection." Case Study, September 2012. *www.dcs.kcl.ac.uk/ staff/richard/BCI_2012.pdf*.

[30] Wilson, Tim. "Report: Nearly 200 Million Records Compromised in Q1." *Information Week*, Dark Reading, May 1, 214AD. *www.darkreading.com/report-nearly-200-million-records-compromised-in-q1/d/d-id/1235010*.

[31] "Ponemon Institute Releases 2014 Cost of Data Breach: Global Analysis." News & Updates, May 5, 2014. *www.ponemon.org/blog/ ponemon-institute-releases-2014-cost-of-data-breach-global-analysis*.

[32] Ibid.

[33] "The Leaky Corporation." The Economist, Companies and information, February 24, 2011. *www.economist.com/node/18226961*.

[34] Lederman, Gordon, and Kate Martin. "The Threat from Within: What Is the Scope of Homegrown Terrorism?" ABA Journal, In-Depth Reporting, July 1, 2012. *www.abajournal.com/magazine/article/the_ threat_from_within_what_is_the_scope_of_homegrown_terrorism/*.

[35] "Insider Threat and Terrorism." Accessed December 7, 2015. *www.knox.army.mil/partners/902d/threat.aspx*.

[36] Bunn, Matthew, and Scott D. Sagan. "A Worst Practices Guide O Insider Threat: Lessons from Past Mistakes." Policy Brief. American Academy of Arts & Sciences, April 1, 2014. *http://cisac.fsi.stanford. edu/publications/worst_practices_guide_to_insider_threats_lessons_ from_past_mistakes/*.

[37] Rules. *Brainy Quote*. Accessed October 13, 2015. *www.brainyquote.com/ search_results.html?q=breaking+rules*

[38] Ibid.

[39] "Pentagon: Afghanistan Insider Threat 'Pernicious'." *BBC News*, August 5, 2014, sec. Asia. *www.bbc.com/news/world-asia-28667424*.

[40] Stewart, Phillip. "Role of the U.S. Government in Industrial Espionage." Research Report. Industrial College of the Armed Forces, April 1994. *http://oai.dtic.mil/oai/oai?&verb=getRecord&metadata Prefix=html&identifier=ADA288212*.

[41] Prados, John. "The John Walker Spy Ring and The U.S. Navy's Biggest Betrayal." *Naval History Magazine* 24, no. 3 (June 2010). *www.usni.org/magazines/navalhistory/2010-06/navys-biggest-betrayal.*
[42] Davidson, Jean. "O.C. Soldier Led Unusual Life : Peri as Spy: Unbelievable to Those Who Knew Him." *Los Angeles Times*, June 27, 1986, sec. Collections - Army (U.S.) - Personnel. *http://articles.latimes.com/1989-06-27/news/mn-4496_1_winnie-peri-east-germany-michael-peri.*
[43] "Robert Phillip Hanssen Espionage Case: Statement of FBI Director Louis J. Freeh On the Arrest of FBI Special Agent Robert Phillip Hanssen." Press Release. U.S. Federal Bureau of Investigation, February 20, 2001. *www.fbi.gov/about-us/history/famous-cases/robert-hanssen.*
[44] Ibid.
[45] Ibid.
[46] Prados, John.
[47] Ibid.
[48] Ibid.
[49] "CPNI Insider Data Collection: Report of Main Findings." Centre for the Protection of National Infrastructure, April 2013. *www.cpni.gov.uk/advice/personnel-security1/insider-threats/.*
[50] Ibid., 20.
[51] Charney, Dr. D.L., Page 48.
[52] Harding, Luke. *The Snowden Files: The Inside Story of the World's Most Wanted Man.* New York, NY: Vintage Books, 2014.
[53] Capelli, Dawn, Akash G. Desali, Andrew P. Moore, Timothy Shimeall, Elise A. Weaver, and Bradford J. Wilke. "Management and Education of the Risk of Insider Threat (MERIT): Mitigating the Risk of Sabotage to Employers' Information, Systems or Networks." Technical Note. Pittsburgh, Pennsylvania: Carnegie Mellon Software Engineering Institute, March 2007. *http://resources.sei.cmu.edu/library/asset-view.cfm?assetID=8031.*
[54] "CPNI Insider Data Collection Study: Report of Main Findings." Center for the Protection of National Infrastructure, April 2013.
[55] Charney, 48-49.
[56] Ibid., 49.
[57] Ibid., 50.
[58] Hattem, Julian. "Snowden: 'To do the right thing you have to break the law." *The Hill*, May 28, 2014, sec. Home|Policy|Technology.

http://thehill.com/policy/technology/207521-defiant-snowden-to-do-the-right-thing-you-have-to-break-the-law.
[59] Insider Threat and Terrorism.
[60] "CPNI Insider Data Collection: Report of Main Findings."
[61] Greitzer, Frank L., Patrick R. Paulson, Lars J. Kangas, Lyndsey R. Franklin, Thomas W. Edgar, and Deborah A. Frincke. "Predictive Modeling for Insider Threat." U.S. Department of Energy, April 2009. *www.pnl.gov/cogInformatics/media/pdf/TR-PACMAN-65204.pdf.* 2.
[62] Ibid., 3.
[63] Band, D. R., Dawn Capelli, L. F. Fischer, Andrew P. Moore, Eric D. Shaw, and Randall Trzeciak. "Comparing Insider IT Sabotate and Espionage: A Model-Based Analysis." Carnegie Mellon Software Engineering Institute, 2006.
[64] Intentional Actions. *Brainy Quote.* Accessed October 13, 2015. *www.brainyquote.com/search_results.html?q=unintentional*
[65] Chickowski, Ericka. "Insider Security Events Mostly Unintentional." *Channelinsider*, August 25, 2009, sec. Security. *www.channelinsider.com/c/a/Security/Insider-Security-Events-Mostly-Unintentional-838558.*
[66] Mundie, David. "Unintentional Insider Threats: The Non-Malicious Within." *Insider Threat Blog*, August 7, 2013. *https://insights.sei.cmu.edu/insider-threat/2013/08/-unintentional-insider-threats-the-non-malicious-within.html*
[67] Greitzer, Frank L., Jeremy R. Strozer, Sholom Cohen, Andrew P. Moore, David Mundie, and Jennifer Cowley. "Analysis of Unintentional Insider Threats Deriving from Social Engineering," 2014. doi:10.1109/SPW.2014.39.
[68] "The New Phishing Threat: Phishing Attack." White Paper. Sunnydale, CA: Proofpoint, 2012.
[69] Colson, Shay C. "Insider Threats 2.0: The Oblivious Insider: A Case Study." Syracuse University School of Information Studies, Spring 2009.
[70] Kendall, Sandy. "NWW: First Case of 'Drive-By Pharming' Identified." *Chief Security Officer (CSO)*, News, January 23, 2008. *www.csoonline.com/article/2122532/build-ci-sdlc/nww--first-case-of--drive-by-pharming--identified-in-the-wild.html.*
[71] Armstrong, Colin. "Mapping Social Media Insider Threat Attack Vectors." Hawaii: Curtin University of Technology, 2013. doi:10.1109/HICSS.2013.392, 1840.
[72] Ibid., 1843.

[73] Cloud Computing. *Brainy Quote*. Accessed October 13, 2015. *www.brainyquote.com/search_results.html?q=cloud+computing*

[74] Kellett, Andrew. "2015 Vormetric Insider Threat Report: Trends and Future Directions in Data Security." Vormetric Data Security, 2015. *www.vormetric.com/campaigns/insiderthreat/2015/.*

[75] Laney, Doug. "3D Data Management: Controlling Data Volume, Velocity, and Variety," February 6, 2001. *http://blogs.gartner.com/ doug-laney/files/2012/01/ad949-3D-Data-Management-Controlling-Data-Volume-Velocity-and-Variety.pdf.*

[76] Tucker, Patrick. "How Big Data Could Help the U.S. Predict the Next Snowden." *Defense One*, February 12, 2014. *www.defenseone.com/ technology/2014/02/how-big-data-could-help-us-predict-next-snowden/ 78671/.*

[77] Brandon, Jonathan. "Three Years after US 'Cloud First' Mandate, Federal Agencies Struggle with Implementation." *Business Cloud News*, February 10, 2014. Accessed December 3, 2015. *www.businesscloudnews.com/2014/02/10/three-years-after-us-cloud-first-mandate-federal-agencies-struggle-with-implementation/*

[78] Claycomb, William R., and Alex Nicoll. "Insider Threats to Cloud Computing: Directions for New Research Challenges." White Paper. Pittsburgh, Pennsylvania: Carnegie Mellon Software Engineering Institute, July 1, 2012. *http://resources.sei.cmu.edu/asset_files/ WhitePaper/2012_019_001_52385.pdf.*

[79] Ibid.

[80] Ibid.

[81] NIST Big Data Public Working Group. "NIST Big Data Interoperability Framework: Volume 4, Security and Privacy." Special Publication. NIST Big Data Interoperability Framework. National Institute of Standards and Technology, September 2015.

[82] Ibid., 8.

[83] Different Perspectives. *Brainy Quote*. Accessed October 13, 2015. *www.brainyquote.com/search_results.html?q=+different+perspectives &pg=1*

[84] Colwill, Carl. "Human Factors in Information Security: The Insider Threat - Who Can You Trust These Days?" Information Security Technical Report. ScienceDirect, 2009. *http://csb.uncw.edu/people/ cummingsj/classes/MIS534/Articles/Ch11InternalThreatsUsers.pdf.*

[85] Kellett.

[86] Flynn, Lori, Carly Huth, Palma Buttles-Valdez, Michael Theis, George Silowash, Tracy Cassidy, Travis Wright, and Randall Trzeciak.

"International Implementation of Best Practices for Mitigating Insider Threat: Analyses for India and Germany." Technical Report. Carnegie Mellon Software Engineering Institute, April 2014. *www.sei.cmu.edu.*
[87] Colwill, 191.
[88] Kellet, 12.
[89] Ibid., 12.
[90] Ibid., 16
[91] Flynn, et.al, 37.
[92] Ibid., 14.
[93] Ibid., 17.
[94] Kellet, 17.
[95] Winsor, Ben. "Here's What Radical Islam Looks Like in the UK." *Business Insider*, August 29, 2014, sec. Military and Defense. *www.businessinsider.com/what-radical-islam-looks-like-in-the-uk-2014-8.*
[96] Flynn, et.al, 12.
[97] Levine, Lawrence A. "Evidence Points to Insider Threat in Downing of Russian Jet." *The World Post*, November 20, 2015, U.S. Edition. *www.huffingtonpost.com/lawrence-a-levine/evidence-points-to-insider-threat_b_8593686.html.*
[98] Best Practices. *Brainy Quote.* Accessed October 13, 2015. *www.bing.com/search?q=marcus+buckingham&form=PRUSEN&mkt=enus&refig=19d527be114348e1b990d491a9e4cee8&ghc=1&filters=ufn%3A%22marcus+buckingham%22+sid%3A%22e074da62-d7d4-d637-d3b1-8862abd3a6b8%22&qs=MB&pq=marcus+buckin&sc=8-13&sp=1&cvid=19d527be114348e1b990d491a9e4cee8*
[99] Cyber Council: Insider Threat Task Force. "A Preliminary Examination of Insider Threat in the U.S. Private Sector." Intelligence and National Security Alliance (INSA), September 2013. *www.insaonline.org.*
[100] Cyber Council: Insider Threat Task Force, 5.
[101] "The Risk of Insider Fraud: Second Annual Study." Annual Study. Ponemon Institute LLC, February 2013.
[102] Collins, Matt. "InTP Series: Key Elements of an Insider Threat Program (Part 2 of 18)." *Insider Threat Blog.* Accessed January 5, 2016. *https://insights.sei.cmu.edu/insider-threat/2015/03/intp-series-key-elements-of-an-insider-threat-program-part-3-of-18.html.*
[103] Collins, Matt. "InTP Series: Key Elements of an Insider Threat Program (Part 2 of 18)." *Insider Threat Blog.* Accessed January 5,

2016. *https://insights.sei.cmu.edu/insider-threat/2015/03/intp-series-key-elements-of-an-insider-threat-program-part-2-of-18.html*.
[104] Insider Threat Integrated Process Team. "DoD Insider Threat Mitigation: Final Report." Information Assurance Technology Analysis Center (IATAC), September 20, 2015, 7.
[105] Allen, Julia H. "How Much Security Is Enough?" Carnegie Mellon Software Engineering Institute, November 30, 2009. *https://buildsecurityin.us-cert.gov/articles/best-practices/governance-and-management/how-much-security-is-enough*.
[106] Berra, Yogi. "Yogi Berra Quotes." *Things People Said*. Accessed December 3, 2015. *http://rinkworks.com/said/yogiberra.shtml*.
[107] Bartol, Nadya, Brian Bates, Karen Mercedes Goertzel, and Theodore Winograd. "Measuring Cyber Security and Information Assurance." State-of-the-Art Report. Information Assurance Technology Analysis Center (IATAC), May 2009.
[108] Ayoub, Robert. "Analysis of Business-Driven Metrics: Measuring for Security Value." DM Review, March 2006. *www.researchgate.net/publication/267205662_Information_Security_Metrics_Research_Directions*.
[109] Chew, Elizabeth, Nadya Barton, Marianne Swanson, Kevin Stine, Anthony Brown, and Will Robinson. "NIST Special Publication 800-55 Revision 1: Performance Measures for Information Systems." National Institute of Standards and Technology, July 2008. *http://csrc.nist.gov/publications/nistpubs/800-55-Rev1/SP800-55-rev1.pdf*.
[110] Capelli, Desali, et al., 18-19.
[111] Schein, Edgar H. *The Corporate Culture Survival Guide*. New and Revised Edition. San Francisco, CA: John Wiley & Sons, 2009.
[112] "Star Trek: Borg Quotes." *GreatQuotes*. Accessed January 15, 2016. *www.great-quotes.com/quotes/movie/Star+Trek:+Borg*.
[113] Silowash, et. al., 17.
[114] Condon, Ron. "Background Employment Screening Decreases Insider Threat, Study Says." *ComputerWeekly.com*, August 2, 2010. *www.computerweekly.com/news/1517261/Background-employment-screening-decreases-insider-threats-study-says*.
[115] International Organization for Standardization (ISO). "ISO/IEC 27001:2013(en): Information Technology - Security Techniques - Information Security Management Systems - Requirements." International Organization for Standardization (ISO), n.d. *www.iso.org/obp/ui/#iso:std:iso-iec:27001:ed-2:v1:en*.
[116] Ibid.

End Notes

[117] Taylor, Paul. J., Linden J. Ball, Coral J. Dando, Thomas C. Ormerod, Marisa C. Jenkins, Alexandra Sandham, and Tarek Manacere. "Detecting Insider Threats Through Language Changes." *Law and Human Behavior* Vol. 37, no. 4 (June 10, 2013): 267–75.

[118] Moore, et.al.

[119] Taylor, et.al., 268.

[120] Ibid., 268.

[121] Armstrong, 1840.

[122] "Facebook Statistics." *Statistic Brain Research Institute*, September 20, 2015. *www.statisticbrain.com/facebook-statistics/*.

[123] Mariotti, John. "The Explosion of Social Media: Blessing or Curse?" *American Express OPENforum*, February 10, 2012. *www.americanexpress.com/us/small-business/openforum/articles/the-explosion-of-social-media-blessing-or-curse/*.

[124] Silowash, et. al., 87.

[125] Carmon, Yigil, and Steven Stalinsky. "Terrorist Use of U.S. Social Media Is a National Security Threat." *Forbes*, January 30, 2015. *www.forbes.com/sites/realspin/2015/01/30/terrorist-use-of-u-s-social-media-is-a-national-security-threat/#2715e4857a0b31cc76b112d0*.

[126] Gegick, Michael, and Sean Barnum. "Least Privilege." Cigital, September 14, 2005. *https://buildsecurityin.us-cert.gov/articles/knowledge/principles/least-privilege*.

[127] Silowash, et.al., 40.

[128] Lohrey, Jackie. "eHow Discover." *eHow*. Accessed January 25, 2016. *www.ehow.com/list_6122703_internal-controls-segregation-duties.html*.

[129] Gegick and Barnum., 32.

[130] "Employee Tenure Summary." Economic News Release. U.S. Bureau of Labor Statistics, September 18, 2014. *www.bls.gov/news.release/tenure.nr0.htm*.

[131] Silowash, et.al., 9.

[132] Weiland, Robert, Andrew P. Moore, Dawn Cappelli, Randall Trzeciak, and Derrick Spooner. "Spotlight On: Insider Threat from Trusted Business Partners." Carnegie Mellon Software Engineering Institute, February 2010. *http://resources.sei.cmu.edu/asset_files/WhitePaper/2010_019_001_52368.pdf*.

[133] Perrin, Chad. "Understanding Layered Security and Defense in Depth." *TechRepublic*, Security, December 18, 2008. *www.techrepublic.com/blog/it-security/understanding-layered-security-and-defense-in-depth/*.

[134] Insider Threat Integrated Process Team.

[135] Montelibano, Joji, and Andrew Moore. "Insider Threat Reference Architecture." Technical Report. Carnegie Mellon Software Engineering Institute, April 2012. *www.sei.cmu.edu*.

[136] "Top 10 Hacker Tools." *AltiusIT*. Accessed January 5, 2016. *www.altiusit.com/files/blog/Top10HackerTools.htm*.

[137] Capelli, Dawn, Andrew P. Moore, Timothy Shimeall, and Randall Trzeciak. "Common Sense Guide to Prevention and Detection of Insider Threats. 2nd Edition." Carnegie Mellon Software Engineering Institute, July 2008.

[138] Weber, Chris and Gary Bahudar. "Wireless Networking Security." *https://technet.microsoft.com/en-us/library/bb457019.aspx*

[139] Mell, Peter, and Timothy Grance. "Special Publication 800-145, The NIST Definition of Cloud Computing." National Institute of Standards and Technology, 2011.

[140] Silowash, et.al., 57.

[141] "Cyber-Security Risks in the Supply Chain." Computer Emergency Reponse Team - United Kingdom (CERT-UK), 2015. *www.cert.gov.uk/wp-content/uploads/2015/02/Cyber-security-risks-in-the-supply-chain.pdf*.

[142] Ibid.

[143] Bunn and Sagan.

[144] Ibid., 7.

[145] Harrell, Eben. "We're Not Prepared for a Nuclear Heist." *Time Magazine Online*, Opinion: Global Security, March 24, 2014. *http://time.com/33802/were-not-prepared-for-a-nuclear-heist/*.

[146] Bunn and Sagan, 14.

[147] Johnson, Dr. Roger G. "Security Maxims." Argonne National Laboratory, September 2013.

[148] Adams, Creighton. "Creighton Adams Quotes." *Brainy Quote*. Accessed January 15, 2016. *www.brainyquote.com/quotes/quotes/c/creightona207381.html*.

ITG RESOURCES

IT Governance Ltd sources, creates and delivers products and services to meet the real-world, evolving IT governance needs of today's organisations, directors, managers and practitioners.

The ITG website (www.itgovernance.co.uk) is the international one-stop-shop for corporate and IT governance information, advice, guidance, books, tools, training and consultancy. On the website you will find the following page related to the subject matter of this book:

www.itgovernance.co.uk/infosec.aspx

Publishing Services

IT Governance Publishing (ITGP) is the world's leading IT-GRC publishing imprint that is wholly owned by IT Governance Ltd.

With books and tools covering all IT governance, risk and compliance frameworks, we are the publisher of choice for authors and distributors alike, producing unique and practical publications of the highest quality, in the latest formats available, which readers will find invaluable.

www.itgovernancepublishing.co.uk is the website dedicated to ITGP. Other titles published by ITGP that may be of interest include:

- CyberWar, CyberTerror, CyberCrime and CyberActivism

  www.itgovernance.co.uk/shop/p-511.aspx

- Information Security: A Practical Guide

  www.itgovernance.co.uk/shop/p-1701.aspx

- The Psychology of Information Security

ITG Resources

www.itgovernance.co.uk/shop/p-1793.aspx

We also offer a range of off-the-shelf toolkits that give comprehensive, customisable documents to help users create the specific documentation they need to properly implement a management system or standard. Written by experienced practitioners and based on the latest best practice, ITGP toolkits can save months of work for organisations working towards compliance with a given standard.

Please visit *www.itgovernance.co.uk/shop/c-129-toolkits.aspx* to see our full range of toolkits.

Training Services

Staff training is an essential component of the information security triad of people, processes and technology. IT Governance's ISO27001 Learning Pathway provides information security courses from Foundation to Advanced level, with qualifications awarded by IBITGQ.

Many courses are available in Live Online as well as classroom formats, so delegates can learn and achieve essential career progression from the comfort of their own homes and offices. Delegates passing the exams associated with our ISO27001 Learning Pathway will gain qualifications from IBITGQ, including CIS F, CIS IA, CIS LI, CIS LA, CIS RM and CIS 2013 UP.

For more information about IT Governance's ISO27001 Learning Pathway, please see:

www.itgovernance.co.uk/iso27001-information-security-training.aspx.

Professional Services and Consultancy

Implementing, maintaining and continually improving an information security management system (ISMS) can be confusing. Companies that focus solely on compliance without appropriately tailoring their security policies to their business needs frequently find their efforts actually provide a poor return on investment: employees can come under strain when poorly implemented security controls prevent them from performing their core business tasks, forcing them to find ways of circumventing security measures, and putting the company at risk.

Fortunately, IT Governance's consultants offer a comprehensive range of flexible, practical project support packages to help organisations of any size, sector or location to implement an ISMS appropriate to their needs while achieving certification to ISO 27001.

For more information on our ISO 27001 consultancy service, please see:

www.itgovernance.co.uk/iso27001_consultancy.aspx.

For general information about our other consultancy services, including for ISO 20000, ISO 22301, Cyber Essentials, the PCI DSS, data protection and more, please see: *www.itgovernance.co.uk/consulting.aspx*.

Newsletter

You can stay up to date with the latest developments across the whole spectrum of IT governance subject matter, including risk management, information security, ITIL and IT service management, project governance, compliance and so much more, by subscribing to our newsletter.

Simply visit our subscription centre and select your preferences:

www.itgovernance.co.uk/newsletter.aspx.